IS THERE LIFE IN OTHER WORLDS?

Poul Anderson

SAUCERIAN PUBLISHER

ISBN: **978-1-955087-15-5**

9 781955 087155

Poul Anderson

Prologue

Poul Anderson was born on November 25, 1926, in Bristol, Pennsylvania, of Scandinavian parents. Shortly after his birth, his father, Anton Anderson, an engineer, moved the family to Texas, where they lived for over ten years. Following Anton Anderson's death, his widow took her children to Denmark. The family returned to the United States after the outbreak of World War II, settling eventually on a Minnesota farm.

Poul Anderson was one of the most prolific and popular writers in science fiction. He won the Hugo Award seven times and the Nebula Award three times, as well as many other awards, notably including the Grand Master Award of the Science Fiction Writers of America for a lifetime of distinguished achievement. With a degree in physics, and a wide knowledge of other fields of science, he was noted for building stories on a solid foundation of real science, as well as for being one of the most skilled creators of fast-paced adventure stories. He was author of over a hundred novels and story collections, and several hundred short stories, as well as several mysteries and non-fiction books. ysteries and non-fiction books. He died in 2001.

Saucerian Publisher was founded with the mission of promoting books in Science Fiction, Paranormal and the Occult. Our vision is to preserve the legacy of literary history by reprint editions of books which have already been exhausted or are difficult to obtain. Our goal is to help readers, educators and researchers by bringing back original publications that are difficult to find at reasonable price, while preserving the legacy of universal knowledge. **IMPORTANT**:This book is an authentic reproduction of the original printed text in shades of gray and may contain minor errors. Despite the fact that we have attempted to accurately maintain the integrity of the original work, the present reproduction may have minor errors beyond our control like: missing and blurred pages, poor pictures and markings. Because this book is culturally important, we have made available as part of our commitment to protect, preserve and promote knowledge in the world. 'This title was originally published in 1963.

Editor
Saucerian Publisher, 2022

Is There Life on Other Worlds?

POUL ANDERSON

With an Introduction by Isaac Asimov

Introduction

THERE IS AN INHERENT FASCINATION in trying to penetrate the unknown. What could possibly have interested Pandora more than a locked box she was forbidden to open? When Bluebeard instructed his wife that she might open every room in the house but one, did he not know which would be the only room she would die to enter?

For that matter, when the Lord God commanded Adam, saying, "Of every tree of the garden thou mayest freely eat: But of the tree of the knowledge of good and evil, thou shalt not eat of it . . ., " surely He must have known that man being man, the fruit of that tree would be eaten as soon as He turned His back.

All of us are Pandoras and Bluebeard's wives and Adams, and this is true of scientists most of all. Chemists have surrounded themselves with poisonous fumes, physicists with all-but-sure electrocution, biologists with virulently toxic bacteria, and all counted the risks small if they were but given a fair chance at wresting even one infinitesimal sliver of the unknown out of the grasp of the universe and bringing it out to the light of common understanding.

Increasing knowledge has vastly increased the volume of the unknown and therefore of the excitement of science. The unknown of the subatomic world looms darkly before the cyclotrons, but the ancients did not know the subatomic world existed and therefore did not know it contained mysteries. The inner structure of the nucleic acid molecule, the fascinating properties of matter at temperatures near absolute zero, the wonder of the cosmic ray and the neutrino—all meant nothing to the wisest Greek philosopher. He lacked any feeling of ignorance about these matters for they did not exist for him.

But one vast mystery unites us with the ancient philosophers and, indeed, with all of mankind back to the first apeman who stared open-mouthed and with the barest beginning of wonder at the stars. It is the mystery of the dark night sky and the bright points of stars, of what they are and what they do and what they imply.

That same mystery looms before us today. The vastness of space hovers over us and engulfs us and reduces all our massive increase in astronomical learning to nothing. As the seven lean kine of Pharaoh's dream devoured the seven fat kine and yet remained as thin as before, so the gigantic question mark of the universe absorbs all we have discovered and remains as great a question mark as before.

We now have instruments that can detect the energy flux between the stars—types of energy of which the greatest physicists, a century ago, never dreamed. We now have vessels that can carry men beyond the atmosphere and, almost, to the Moon.

Yet that but intensifies the question mark and makes it larger, not smaller. For if we can "hear" the radio waves of the universe, what may we not "hear" if we listen closely? And if we stand on the alien dust of other worlds, what may we not stumble over as we walk?

The questions that but a few years ago we would have been half-ashamed to ask we now *must* ask. Are we alone? If life exists here, may it not exist elsewhere? If intelligence exists here, may it not exist elsewhere? If man exists here, may he not (at least in the form of an unreasonable facsimile) exist elsewhere?

This represents the speculative birth of a new science: astrobiology—the study of life outside the earth.

There can be no accurate knowledge of astrobiology without first an understanding of astronomy and astrophysics and astrochemistry, for these sciences supply the necessary background information for a proper conception of the manner in which the distant life on other worlds must play itself out. To write a book on the subject of such other-life requires a good grasp of the physical sciences, and this Poul Anderson has.

But he has more, much more. There are many who have

the necessary grasp of the sciences but considerably fewer who have the necessary grasp *and* the ability to write clearly and dramatically.

And surely there are very few who have the necessary grasp and the necessary writing ability *and* the sternly disciplined imagination that can pour light on hidden corners where no hard evidence yet exists, without allowing the light to waste itself uselessly in an empty spiral of meaningless maybes.

Poul Anderson's imagination was developed in a hard and superlatively effective school, for he is one of the handful of serious science fiction writers who have made that segment of literature a respected field in this last generation.

To the book now in your hands—not science fiction at all, but a kind of sober science that is yet as exciting and fresh as science fiction itself—Poul Anderson brings not only the sober consideration of what scientists believe to be fact but also carefully culled specimens of speculation beyond the actual fact by men who have been thinking hard about the problem of other-life for decades. Best of all, he has added considerable stimulating speculation of his own.

I feel certain that no one who reads this book will ever look up at the stars without a twinge of wonder of a kind he never felt before.

—Isaac Asimov

Contents

Foreword

THE DREAM is old that men might someday reach beyond this Earth, walk on other planets, and speak with those who dwell there. Already, in A.D. 160, Lucian of Samosata fabled about voyages to the Moon. But then the dream lay fourteen centuries fallow, until Copernicus of Thorn re-created the concept, which Greek Aristarchus had had about 280 B.C., that our world is one among the planets, all circling the Sun. The work of Tycho, Galileo, Kepler, and Newton followed, establishing the idea so firmly that today it is the Earth-centered Ptolemaic system that seems unthinkable. And so the wish was revived to explore the heavens, not by peering through a cloudy atmosphere and across multiple millions of miles but in the way of Columbus.

Great names are attached to some of the interplanetary romances: Kepler himself, Cyrano de Bergerac, Voltaire, Dumas. Many were written only for philosophical or satirical purposes, as Jonathan Swift described imaginary lands in distant seas. But others were, to a degree at least, serious attempts to imagine what other globes might be like. The books of Jules Verne, Kurd Lasswitz, and H. G. Wells are probably the best known in this tradition, which has remained very much alive to the present day.

Meanwhile science itself gathered facts and built theories about the planets and the stars beyond them. The means of travel within the Solar System were investigated mathematically by such men as Ziolkovsky and Oberth, experimentally by such as Goddard and the old *Verein für Raumschiffahrt* (Society for Space Travel). Well before 1940, their studies had gone so far that the problem looked simply like one of engineering development, dependent on little more than raising the enormous funds required. But this, in turn, meant convincing enough people that interplanetary voyaging was an attainable and desirable goal.

There is no need to relate here the ironic story of how the work was begun otherwise, because of a war and the armed truce that followed. Irony is, after all, the one universal quality of human existence. Nor need I relate how spacefaring has turned out to demand research more fundamental than a team of engineers can do, how the project is in fact calling on every intellectual resource we have. Other books deal with these matters. For us, here and now, it is sufficient that man is on his way.

To most people the realization came with shocking suddenness. Though talk about long-range passenger rockets grew respectable after 1945, it was regarded by the public as largely talk—a moderately interesting item in the popular science reports, a vague future possibility that, if it ever came to pass, would mean no more in daily life than an expedition to the South Pole. But then on October 4, 1957, the first Sputnik went up. And all at once men saw the thing in the sky, over their own personal heads.

Even those of us who had lived with the dream for a good part of our lives found that an eerie moment, as we stood in the cold before sunrise and watched a new star hurtle among the fading constellations. Since then the pace has mounted. Each year, more men come home to tell how they orbited the world; artificial meteoroids have crashed on the Moon, on Venus, perhaps on Mars; images of Luna's far side have been sent us, lands never seen before in Earth's whole history; vehicles have begun to descend with instruments to analyze the surface and radio back the composition of Lunar rock. Meanwhile other automatic vessels have passed by Venus and Mars and sent back some astonishing information. I have watched literally hundreds of dark-suited, crew-cut organization men listen to lengthy technical discussions of how they can best put a manned base on the Moon. Well before this century is out, human footsteps should also have marked at least two other planets.

And yet the implications are still not generally understood.

Space flight is usually considered a mere expensive race for military advantage and propaganda kudos. To a certain extent this is true, unfortunately, and the undertaking can be attacked on that ground. Some distinguished scientists argue that for the same price we could accomplish far more at home, both in building up our strength and in advancing our knowledge. A few telemetric probes, they say, can tell us as much about the Solar System as we will ever need to know.

The argument is wrong. Militarily, the engineering data that will be picked up in the course of this project are crucial—not to mention the likelihood of learning things we do not suspect at present. As for astronomical research, let us never forget that each planet out there, no matter how barren, is a world infinitely complex and mysterious. No instruments, no television cameras can give us more than a few maddening hints.

Beyond these practical considerations there lies the human need for adventure, challenge, and pride in achievement. Men will go beyond our sky as they have gone beyond other horizons in the past—because they are men. And because the curve of technological progress is growing constantly steeper, they will do so much sooner than we really expect.

It seems time, then, to make a few guesses as to what may come of all this effort. If nothing else, we need an idea of how far it is wise to pursue the dream, and why. On the one hand, we are scarcely going to find ourselves in a Buck Rogers situation of beautiful extra-terrestrial princesses and ravenous bug-eyed monsters. On the other hand, space travel means more than a few heroic expeditions and an enlargement of our scientific understanding. The future may well record it as the most important step man took since he invented agriculture, or even since an unknown half-man first tamed fire. We are citizens of the universe. We are about to discover that truth, not as an abstract philosophical proposition but as a living reality. The effect on us will be as profound as the effects of those discoveries made by Copernicus, Darwin, and Freud—or by Gautama Buddha, Confucius, Socrates, and the prophets of Israel.

There has already been some anticipation of the event, a

mental scouting in advance of the reality. In this book I shall bring together those ideas that seem to me the most fruitful, with a few of my own. At our present stage we cannot be certain about very much outside this one planet. But we do have enough information to think seriously about the entire cosmos and our destiny in it.

The first few chapters will try to describe briefly what is known today and what may reasonably be surmised. (References to the sources of new or controversial material are numbered and collected at the back of the book.) Many excellent works already deal with these matters. But they stop where we shall just be starting, at the border line of speculation. By this I do not mean haphazard fancy; rather, a disciplined consideration of what we can be sure does *not* exist anywhere in space, and what probably does exist, and some of the imaginative possibilities that cannot be ignored. In the end we shall ask what our own relationship to the universe may be, now and in the future.

Of course, much of what is said will prove wildly wrong—probably because of having been too conservative rather than too radical. Today we are barely able to ask meaningful questions, and must not expect final answers. Yet we can make a preliminary sketch of the living universe, one that may have to be changed entirely as our knowledge grows, but on which we can base our further thinking and our hopes.

Acknowledgments

IN A BOOK that draws upon the work of many people in several different fields, it is impossible to cite everyone whom the author owes an intellectual debt. But I would like to mention a few who have been especially helpful. At the 1961 meeting in Denver of the American Association for the Advancement of Science, there was held on December 27 an all-day symposium on "Extraterrestrial Biochemistry and Biology," organized by Charles R. Phillips of the U.S. Army Chemical Corps Biological Laboratories. The several speakers at this symposium were most interesting and informative. Other lectures and discussions, elsewhere at the meeting, proved equally valuable, as will be seen in the list of references.

For personal kindness I must first of all thank my wife, Karen Anderson, and Isaac Asimov, who has so generously contributed the Introduction. Special thanks are also due Halton C. Arp, F. Bordes, Sidney W. Fox, Ervin J. Hawrylewicz, R. S. Richardson, Oliver Saari, Carl Sagan, Harry C. Stubbs, and Harold C. Urey. Without them this book could probably not have been written. Of course, they are not responsible for anything that appears in these pages: all mistakes and misinterpretations are entirely my own.

Beyond the bounds our staring rounds,
   Across the pressing dark,
The children wise of outer skies
   Look hitherward and mark
A light that shifts, a glare that drifts,
   Rekindling thus and thus—
Not all forlorn, for Thou hast borne
   Strange tales to them of us.

—Kipling, *To the True Romance*

IS THERE LIFE ON OTHER WORLDS?

Chapter 1

Stage Setting

THE BEST TIME to see the stars is in the dead of winter on some high mountain peak. Then they flash and glitter across a crystal dark, aswarm in their enormous constellations. Orion and the Great Bear, the Dragon and the Bull, wheeling with an awesome stillness about the celestial pole; the Milky Way is like a cataract of ice, the coldest sight in the world. But this is not when I feel their reality the most. That happens in summer, camped out, when I look from my sleeping bag straight skyward and think with a touch of dread how far up my vision is falling. One almost digs fingers into the ground, as if to keep from being thrown off this whirling tiny ball to tumble forever between the stars.

The sensation must be peculiar to men of our era. However wonderful he found the sight, prescientific man could never have conceived of the true vastness of the universe. There is not actually a large number of stars visible to the naked eye—about twenty-five hundred on the clearest nights. Once above the obscuring atmosphere, we might see two and a half times as many in either half of the celestial sphere, or some twelve thousand in all if we floated free in space: untwinkling diamond points, those we know from Earth almost half again as bright, a glorious vision, but still scarcely a glimpse of what our instruments have revealed.

The human mind is not at home with astronomical magnitudes. Since they cannot be comprehended, in the sense that everyday quantities can be, they are often forgotten, or treated with a glibness that avoids any attempt to appreciate what they mean. So let us review the data and put them in our own terms.

The Sun is about ninety-three million miles away. This average distance, known as the astronomical unit, or A.U., makes a convenient yardstick within the Solar System. The mean orbital radii of the planets range from 0.39 A.U. for

Mercury to 35.5 for Pluto. Now suppose a vehicle traveled day and night at an unvarying rate of sixty miles per hour, a mile a minute. To cover one A.U. it would need almost 177 years. It would be reaching Pluto today if it had left the Sun sometime before the dawn of recorded history.

Light, traveling at 186,272 miles per second from the Sun, reaches Earth in a trifle over eight minutes and Pluto in less than five hours. But so great are the distances between the stars that the smallest useful unit is the light-year, the 5,880 billion miles that light travels in a year. Our sixty-mile-per-hour vehicle would take eleven million years for the same journey.

The nearest known star—after Sol, the Sun—is Alpha Centauri, four and one-third light-years distant. The average separation of stars in our neighborhood is about nine light-years. Near the center of the galaxy they are more crowded, possibly averaging one light-year apart. This is still nearly seven million times the diameter of the Sun. Two men seven or eight thousand miles from each other on an otherwise deserted continent, would be as lonely as two stars in the thronged galactic center. But at a reasonable walking pace of twenty miles a day, the men could join forces in six months or so. The stars, heading straight for each other with the abnormally high relative speed (radial velocity) of fifty miles a second, would not collide for thirty-seven hundred years.

Not that they are small. Our Sun, a fairly typical specimen, has a mass 329,300 times Earth's. Being gaseous, it has no definite size; but the photosphere, the disk we see through a piece of smoked glass, is 865,000 miles wide, with a temperature of 11,000° F. The temperature at the center is believed to be 20,000,000° F. There are other orbs that monstrously surpass these figures.

The Galaxies

As everyone knows, the Milky Way is the multitude of distant stars we see along the equatorial plane of our galaxy, where they occur most thickly. This system comprises some hundred billion individual suns; the actual number may be twice as great. Seen edgewise, the galaxy would resemble a lens 100,000 light-years across, with a central bulge—a nucleus—20,000 light-years in diameter and 6,500 light-years thick at the middle. Radio astronomy has shown that there is, in addition, a layer of stars and tenuous material about 700 light-years thick, spread over this optically detectable disc like icing on a cake. Also, the galaxy is surrounded by an ellipsoidal halo. This is an immense region whose longest axis is equal to the galaxy's own diameter and whose volume is fifty times as great, but that is defined only by a very thinly spread group of faint stars and ionized gas (Fig. 1).

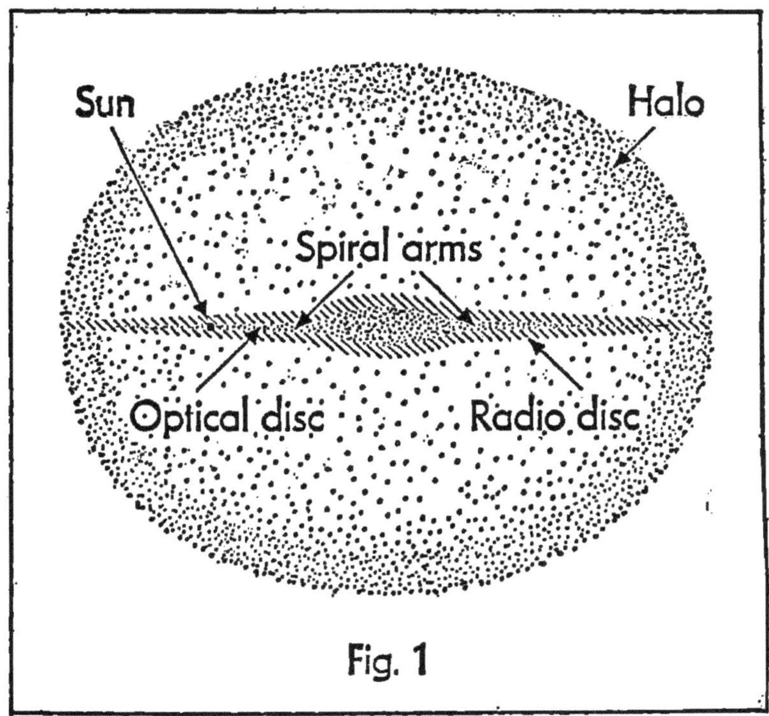

Fig. 1

Observed "from above"—that is, along its axis of rotation —the system would appear more like a huge Catherine wheel than a lens, with several spiral arms curving majestically from a glowing nucleus. We can see this arrangement in photographs of similar galaxies whose planes happen to be tilted toward us (Fig. 2). The space between the arms is comparatively empty, even by interstellar standards. Our Sun lies in one such arm, near its inner edge, about one hundred light-years north of the equatorial plane and almost thirty thousand light-years from the galactic axis. At this distance, and a speed of 130 miles per second, we complete a revolution about the nucleus in approximately 195 million years.

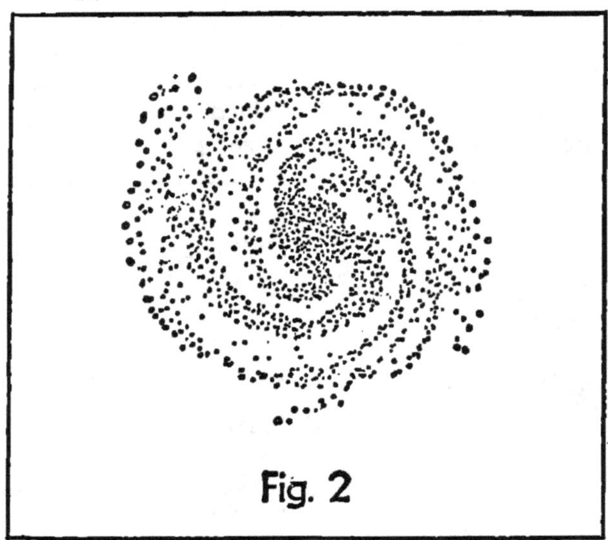

Fig. 2

Of course, there is no sharp edge to the galaxy, any more than there is to a planet's atmosphere. But beyond a certain point the star density drops off rapidly. Most of the mass is concentrated in the nucleus. It lies in the direction of Sagittarius and Ophiuchus and would blaze with radiance were it not surrounded by obscuring clouds of dust. We have seen how much more isolated a star is in our region than near the center. Astronomers in most other galaxies would not even be able to photograph the tenuous rim where we are.

In the night of the Southern Hemisphere, Magellan saw two dim patches of light, which have been named for him, the Magellanic Clouds. These are distinct star groups, 165,000 light-years distant. They are considerably smaller than the Milky Way assemblage—though the larger group is bigger than the average galaxy—and lack its elaborate structure, being of an almost chaotic appearance. Astronomers dispute whether or not they are satellites of our galaxy, but they do have some physical connection with each other and in fact are a single system.[1]

Nearly a million and a half light-years away, in the constellation Andromeda, lies the lovely object catalogued as M31, practically a twin of our galaxy. These two sisters dominate what is called the Local Group, being the largest, brightest, and most massive of its nineteen known members. This cluster of associated galaxies occupies a space more than six million light-years in diameter. Fantastic though such distances are, we can see that the members of a set like this lie closer together, in proportion to their own size, than do the stars within any given system.

Beyond the Local Group the abysses open up, with other clusters separated by millions of light-years. The sheer volume of space would seem to overwhelm them. The conventional estimate of the mean density of matter in the universe—the density if everything that is were spread uniformly through space—is one thousand-billion-billion-billionth gram per cubic centimeter. (Even within our galactic disc, the concentration of the interstellar medium is only a million times greater, or about one hydrogen atom per cubic centimeter. Unusually dense nebulae may be a thousand times again as concentrated, but even they are relatively diffuse. For comparison, one cubic centimeter of hydrogen at standard Terrestrial air pressure and temperature contains a number of atoms expressed by the figure 54 followed by eighteen zeros.)

But despite their inconceivable separation, the galaxies occur in equally inconceivable numbers. The universe is that big. There may be a million million of them within range of the 200-inch telescope on Mount Palomar, which cannot reach to the limits of space. And each contains billions of suns.

Not all galaxies resemble this one. Several classes have been established, but I will only note here the main categories: spiral like ours, irregular like the Magellanic Clouds, and elliptical. Elliptical galaxies, the most common, are typically all but featureless, fainter than the spirals (that is, with fewer really brilliant stars), and contain little or no dust and gas. The irregular galaxies, on the other hand, are generally richer in superbright stars than are the spiral kind.

But we must turn homeward again. This book is not about astrophysics. To us at present, it makes no difference whether space is infinite or, as seems more probable, is finite though unbounded and expanding. Nor need we ponder whether the universe as a whole had a definite beginning and will have a definite end; or goes through an eternal cycle of expansion and contraction; or was always largely the same as it is today and will always remain so. The evidence appears to favor the first of these ideas: that the entire cosmos was born at some time in the past—estimates range from ten billion to twenty billion years ago—and that at some unimaginably remote future time the last generation of stars will have burned out, and the galactic clusters will have receded farther from each other than the last light ray could travel. But even the most guarded estimate of the space and time available to us is, for all human purposes, unlimited.

The Stars

Returning, then, to our own galaxy, let us glance at its myriad individual members. They are wonderfully diverse, and yet they fall into certain well-defined species.

At first this seems hard to believe; it looks as if every thinkable kind of star had been identified. We know red stars like Betelgeuse, with half our Sun's surface temperature but a full 1,200 times as bright because it has 290 times Sol's diameter though less than a millionth of its density. Then there are absolute monsters like Canopus, 80,000 times as radiant as the Sun. (But stars like S Doradus in the Magellanic Cloud system are also known, which give off the light of a million Sols.) There are red dwarfs with a fifth of Sol's mass and a six-hundredth—in some cases, less than a ten-thousandth—of its brightness. There are also dim white dwarfs no bigger than a planet in volume, though the matter in them, collapsed and compressed until a cubic inch holds a ton, remains of stellar quantity. There are several classes of variable stars. Some pulse through regular cycles of luminosity, like the rapid RR Lyrae type with periods of less than a day, the larger Cepheids that may take up to fifty days, or the still slower U Orionis breed. Some flicker irregularly or burst into explosions of the nova sort, an increase in brilliance of thirty thousand to forty thousand times. Novae seem to repeat many times before reaching stability. But the inconceivable catastrophe that produces a supernova can only occur once to a star, when it radiates for days at the rate of 200 million Sols. Some have been known whose peak output exceeded that of their entire galaxy. They may be the source of the cosmic ray particles that sleet through interstellar space and our own bodies.[2]

This is not an exhaustive list of stellar classes, nor do suns alone make up the universe. I have remarked that there is dust and gas between them. Even the densest regions are a hard vacuum by Terrestrial standards. But when such clouds stretch on for light-year after light-year, they block off all view of the stars, and we photograph blacknesses like the Horsehead Nebula or the Coal Sack. The galactic nucleus is virtually hidden from us by the haze around it. Not all nebulae are dark, however. Some, illuminated by hot suns, shine with the delicate beauty of the Veil in Cygnus or the roiled cloudiness in Orion's sword. Thin though it is, the interstellar medium probably equals in mass the totality of the stars.

How shall any order be made of this rich confusion?

One might start by asking how we know what we know. There is not room here to do more than list a very few of the many approaches that have converged in the ideas we hold today.

The distance and hence the absolute brightness of a star can be learned by the familiar method of triangulating from opposite sides of Earth's orbit only if the star lies within a few light-years of us. Greater distances were found for some clusters by analyzing their proper motions. But to measure greater distances yet, less direct means had to be found. For example, it was shown that the period of a Cepheid variable has a definite relationship to its luminosity. So the distance of any Cepheid is obtainable by measuring its period and its apparent magnitude in our sky. The distances of associated stars, like those in the Lesser Magellanic Cloud, can be assumed to be the same without an undue percentage of error. Hence, their brightnesses were also established. On this basis the luminosities of numerous nonvariable types were found.

Now, if a sun has one or more companions, the masses can be calculated from the gravitational effect they are observed to have on each other. A relationship between mass and luminosity was discovered, which fitted many stellar species, if not all. Physical theory confirms our natural belief that it is reasonable to extend this relationship to single stars. From the distribution of radiated wave lengths, surface temperature can be computed. The spectroscope informs us not only about the chemical composition and the state of the atoms in the upper layers but also about rotation and magnetic field. Interferometry has measured the actual diameters of some giants. Lately, radio techniques have opened breathtaking new fields of discovery. Meanwhile a rapidly growing knowledge of nuclear and thermodynamic processes has enabled us to understand, or begin to understand, what goes on within a sun and what the course of its life must be.

In this cat's-cradle fashion, astronomy has built up a considerable body of information. Its methods are more powerful and subtle than this sketch can suggest. Nevertheless, we do well to remember their indirectness and the uncertainty of many important results, especially where other galaxies are concerned.

Sometime before World War I a series of spectral types had been identified and labeled—for historical reasons—O, B, A, F, G, K, M, W, R, N, S.* (All students of astronomy have heard some version of the mnemonic "Oh, be a fine girl, kiss me. Well, right now, sweetheart.") This series, O through M, classifies stars from the very hottest blue ones with surface temperatures of around 80,000 or 90,000° F. to the cool red ones of perhaps 4,500° F. Of course, the range is continuous, so a number from zero through 9 is added to show just where a star lies on the scale. For instance, a K3 is about a third of the way between a K0 and an M0. The Sun is of type G2. Classes W, R, N, and S represent branches in the series with somewhat peculiar conditions and need not concern us here.

When the sequence O through M, essentially a temperature sequence, was plotted against luminosity—each star represented by a point on the chart—a surprisingly simple figure was obtained, not unlike a reversed 7. This is the famous Hertzsprung-Russell diagram (Fig. 3). In general, as might be expected, the hottest stars give off the most radiation, and the mass-luminosity relationship makes them also the heaviest. But one group turns out to be many times more brilliant than

* Actually, this is a modern form of the series. The original one lacked Class W and made the Sun a G0 star.

their color would suggest: the red giants. The reason for this is their enormous size. Antares, for example, is over 400 million miles in diameter. If it were substituted for the Sun, it would swallow the orbit of Mars. In most cases, each square inch of such a star radiates less than does the same area of Sol, but the red giant has a good many more square inches. I have already remarked that this type is not proportionately massive, having, in fact, mean densities that are thousands of times less than that of air.

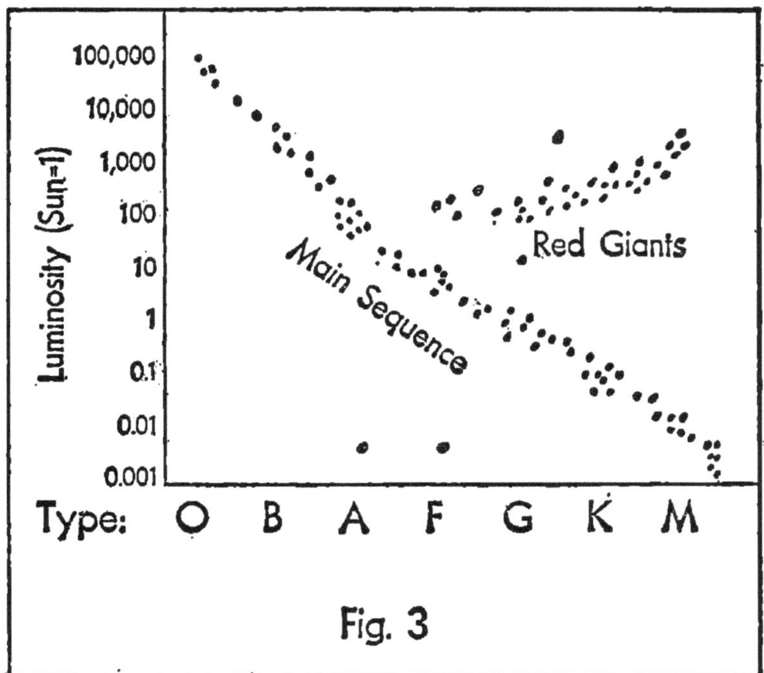

Fig. 3

The diagonal part of the Hertzsprung-Russell diagram is known as the main sequence. Our Sun lies on it, a commonplace yellow dwarf, rather more bright than average. (We shall see that the spectacular blue giants are far outnumbered by the inconspicuous red dwarfs.) In recent years the diagram has become more complicated as new kinds of stars have been discovered. Figure 4 shows some of these classes. We note especially the subdwarfs, paralleling the main sequence with the general characteristics of the Sun, but dimmer in proportion to their temperatures. This may be a spurious class, its spectra made misleading by selective absorption. However, its chemical composition is certainly different from the typical main sequence. Note also the white dwarfs; these are the tiny, incredibly dense stars I have mentioned. The companions of Sirius and Procyon are typical. Elsewhere on the modern diagram we see classes like the supergiants and the variables.

As for the content of the stars, spectroanalysis reveals what the upper layers are like, and theory lets us probe the interior. The exact over-all composition of the Sun is still not entirely known, but an estimate that has wide acceptance makes it not quite 85 per cent hydrogen and 15 per cent helium (in terms of atomic abundance rather than weight). All the remaining elements exist as "impurities," totaling less than 1 per cent. Most other star types have similar though not identical com-

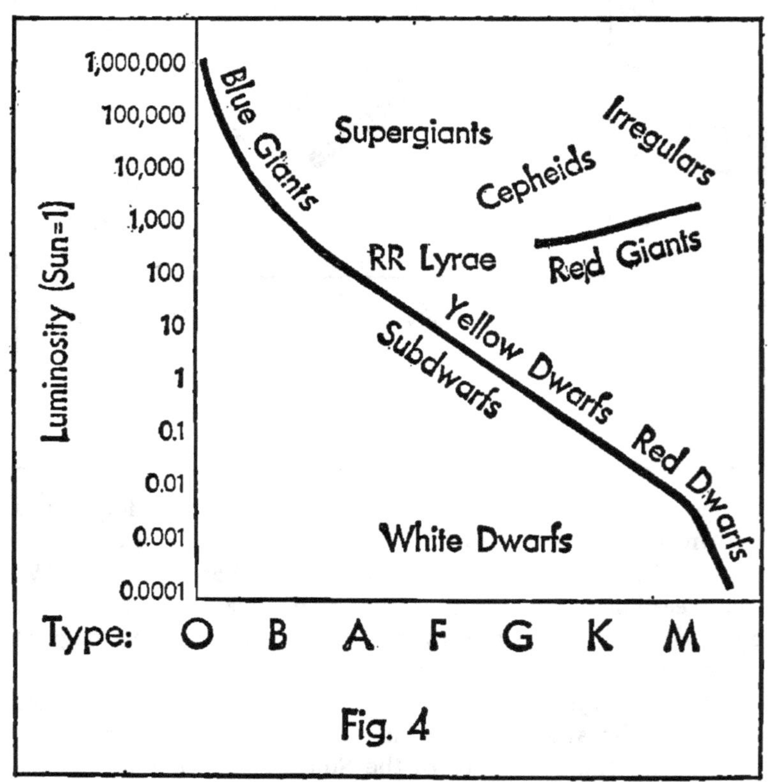

Fig. 4

positions. The interstellar medium appears to be at least 90 per cent hydrogen.

That suggests that this lightest and simplest of the elements is basic to the scheme of things. The principal cosmogonic theories today start with hydrogen alone. Let us make a very brief and incomplete review of what is currently believed about the origin and evolution of the stars. I shall concentrate on the areas of general agreement and bypass, as much as possible, the interesting complications on which the various contending schools base their arguments.

Stellar Evolution

We begin somewhere between ten and twenty billion years ago with a universe that was only a cloud of hydrogen. Its density may have been a hundred times what the average cosmic density is now[3]—but that was still almost a total vacuum "without form and void: and darkness was upon the face of the deep." Nonetheless, the atoms were in random motion and were attracting each other. Over the eons, turbulences and eddies developed. Local concentrations, made by gravitation and statistical fluctuations, shrank and grew denser under the force of their own attraction. As their radii dwindled, their rotation necessarily increased. This helped set up instabilities that caused subunits to coalesce: protogalaxies. Thus the galactic clusters are probably older than their individual members, which in turn are older than the stars that comprise them. Considering the scale of this evolution, immense stretches of time were required; but there was time to spare. Astronomers William A. Fowler and Fred Hoyle believe our own galaxy had become a distinct unit by about fifteen billion years ago.[4] Other authorities make its birth much more recent.

Internal differentiation went on in a similar fashion within each galaxy, until protostars separated out of the medium, sometimes singly, more often in clusters. Every star then proceeded to shrink further and to spin faster. But now the density was high enough that a new process became significant: heating. As the hydrogen atoms fell inward, they gave up energy, just as a waterfall does to a millwheel, and they were compressed. The stars grew incandescent. Some six billion years ago the first lights were kindled. These must have been extremely large bodies, for their strong gravitational fields would hasten the process. According to Halton Arp, a star fifty times as heavy as Sol condenses in a mere ten thousand years.[5] This is about the upper limit. A larger body would be so unstable that it would immediately break up. Smaller stars coalesce at a slower pace.

Temperatures in the highly compressed cores rose to millions of degrees. Under such conditions, thermonuclear reactions began to take place. In a series of nuclear collisions and readjustments, hydrogen was converted to helium, and atomic energy was released. This generated enough internal pressure to halt any further shrinkage. When sufficient helium had been formed, new processes became important, atomic reactions that built up higher elements. We need not trace the series here. In a very massive star it all happened with great rapidity, and after a few million years a catastrophically unstable condition was reached. The star exploded—a supernova—scattering most of its substance back into the interstellar medium. (This is not the only process by which that medium is enriched nowadays.)

Small stars, as I have said, evolve much more slowly. A remnant of the first few generations can still be observed, for example, in the nucleus and halo of spiral galaxies. These dwarf survivors are still dim and very poor in the heavier elements. Walter Baade, who originally identified the class, labeled it Population II, as distinguished from the bright Population I concentrated in the equatorial planes and the arms.

Star formation continued wherever local concentrations of the interstellar medium grew dense enough to coalesce. This process may have been helped along by pressure of light from the suns that already existed, though perhaps hindered by the galaxy's magnetic field. The second generation acquired a very small percentage of those new elements of greater atomic weight than helium that the supernovae had cast into space. Their own thermonuclear reactions and their explosions enriched the insterstellar medium still further, and probably added higher elements than the first generation had been able to form.[6] Eventually, actual particles of dust, containing substances like carbon, oxygen, and the metals, condensed from the interstellar medium.

Galactic rotation tended to concentrate all dust and gas in the spiral arms, where stars are still being born (for example, apparently in the Orion Nebula). Baade's Population I includes the most massive, hence the brightest, of the young stars. Energy spendthrifts, they cannot be very old—the age of Rigel, twenty thousand times as bright as Sol, is calculated as ten million years[7]—nor do they have very long to live. The smaller suns, with less fierce interior conditions, release energy less fast and so have greater life-spans. Nor will they, at the end, become supernovae. The exact course of their evolution depends on such parameters as mass, rotation,[8] and chemical composition. The composition in turn depends greatly on age. The newer a star is, the greater the number of heavy atoms that were available at the time of its formation. However, this is not the only determining factor, for some stars of comparable age differ markedly in content. Probably the metal-poor young ones were formed in parts of the galaxy distant from the equatorial plane and its enriched interstellar material.[9]

Even the most metal-rich stars are composed predominantly of hydrogen and helium. The reader may wonder how a per cent or less of impurity can affect bodies so huge. But 1 per cent of a star still amounts to thousands of Earths. For that matter, the human brain is only about 1 per cent of the total body weight and yet is considered rather influential. By entering into atomic reactions within the star, the heavier elements change the course of its development.

In summary then, the life of a massive sun is brilliant but short. Like all others, it is born out of the interstellar medium. Gravitational attraction compresses it until the nuclear fires are lit and a balance is achieved. A chain of transmutations produces heavier elements. But as the hydrogen supply at the core grows exhausted, the atomic processes move outward. The star leaves the main sequence. If very large, it probably flares up as a supernova. Then, its nuclear resources exhausted, it sinks into the white-dwarf condition, radiating away the energy it can no longer generate. This cooling off is so slow that thus far in the galaxy's history there may be no unshining "black dwarfs" at all.

A smaller star will stay far longer on the main sequence, its position there determined chiefly by its mass. It may change little for billions of years—as much as 100 billion in the case of the M-type dwarfs. But sooner or later it must also move to the right. Our own Sun is expected to become a red giant, so large and brilliant that it will consume its inner planets, including Earth. From that peak, one thousand times its present brightness, it will then cool and contract. The different kinds of variable stars appear to be in stages of transition like this. (Just what main-sequence class gives rise to what sort of variable is as yet uncertain.) Later the waning star may undergo a series of violent adjustments, ordinary nova explosions.* In any event, like the supernovae, it ends as a white dwarf—and so, ultimately, a lightless clinker.

But Sol's death process will not start for a comfortably long time as we reckon such things. According to the best estimates, the date lies five billion years in the future.

Some astronomers think that galaxies have an evolutionary sequence of their own, starting as irregular and proceeding through the spiral form to end as faint reddish elliptical ones.[10] On this view the Magellanic Clouds are younger than our system, at least in comparative age. (As a twenty-year-old man is younger than a twenty-year-old dog.) Others feel that the spiral is normal and that anything different is the result of untoward circumstances, especially galactic collisions. Instances of galaxies encountering each other are known. In such an event, individual stars are not much affected—consider the distances between them—but the interstellar medium certainly is, and no doubt the general galactic structure also.[11] A third idea is that elliptical systems are those that had the least rotation in the beginning, hence little tendency to form spiral arms or to concentrate gas and dust so that stars could be produced in quantity. Thus few if any suns appeared in them after the first generation.[12] Observers agree that the elliptical systems consist almost entirely of Population II. The large proportion of young suns in the irregular galaxies may be just because they are of low mass, so star formation is slow.[13]

* According to another theory, only certain kinds of double stars become novae, and a single star sheds mass less abruptly in its red-giant phase.

This illustrates the many uncertainties that today place astronomy among the most exciting sciences. I should emphasize that the sketch of stellar evolution given here is not only incomplete but controversial. For instance, the bulk of the higher-element atoms may have been formed by the earlier generations of stars rather than more or less continuously as my account has intimated.

Our Sun and Its Neighbors

But for the most part we shall not be concerned with such problems. The smaller main-sequence stars turn out to be those of primary interest to us, and we need no more than a very broad general picture of our galaxy.

Let us therefore recapitulate. In this great Catherine wheel, a hundred thousand light-years across, there are at least a hundred billion suns. Approximately half of them, possibly more, are double. Triple and even more complicated systems are not uncommon. In the dense nucleus of the galaxy, and in the thin halo, lie the older stars. Those small enough not to have burned out may be as much as ten billion years old, cool, reddish, and metal-poor; but many have left the main sequence to become variables, red giants, white dwarfs, and other dying types. Itself largely free of dust and gas, the galactic nucleus is surrounded by dense clouds of interstellar medium, which extend through the spiral arms. Here the younger stars are found and, indeed, star formation continues today. (Of course, there is enough randomness in stellar motions that this segregation by age is not absolute. Ancient suns have wandered outward and young ones inward. But the general distribution is as described.) The newer the star, the richer it tends to be in elements atomically heavier than hydrogen and helium, though composition is also influenced by other factors such as the galactic location in which it happened to condense. The bigger it is, the brighter it shines and the lower its life expectancy.

Our Sun is about four and a half billion years old, a middle-aged dwarf of Class G, slightly more massive and definitely brighter than the average member of the main sequence—but not enough so to be especially noteworthy. It lies far out in a spiral arm, thirty thousand light-years from the center, where the stars have begun to thin away toward emptiness.

Nearly all the stars we normally see are more luminous than the Sun; otherwise we could not see them. At a removal of about fifty-six light-years, Sol would no longer be a naked-eye object. The telescope extends this range, but at great distances the selection in favor of giants becomes operative again. However, there is no reason to doubt that main-sequence dwarfs are common throughout all normal galaxies. A survey of our neighborhood confirms this.

Within a sixteen light-years radius of us, fifty-five stars are known, including Sol. But fewer than a dozen are visible to the unaided eye. Of these fifty-five, there are thirty-one single stars like ours; the rest occur in nine double and two triple systems. The most brilliant is Sirius, twenty-three times as luminous as Sol; the faintest is Wolf 359, with one sixty-thousandth of our Sun's output. Only five of the fifty-five are as bright as ours or brighter, and six have luminosities ranging from less than one to one-tenth that of Sol. The rest are dimmer still. These include five white dwarfs, all the other local residents being on the main sequence. Some exceedingly faint ones may well remain to be discovered.[14]

The Origin of Planets

Sol has a feature that once seemed unique: its family of planets. But today we believe a large fraction, probably a majority of stars have similar companions.

The exact process that gives rise to them is still under debate, and again I can only offer a very broad view. Even then I will find myself at odds with one or another school of thought on this or that detail.

Though the planets collectively have scarcely more than 1 per cent of the mass of the Solar System, they have about 98 per cent of the angular momentum—the "quantity of rotation." This anomaly baffled many earlier attempts to explain their origin, but recent thinkers have made use of it. None of the theories that called the Solar System the result of an accident, such as the near approach of two stars, have survived rigorous analysis. But the general outline of the noncatastrophic concepts makes good physical sense.

As the mass of dust and gas that is a protostar contracts, it spins faster and faster. If the star is big enough, this action may break it up into two or more roughly comparable masses, and so form a multiple star.[15] (This idea is not universally accepted among astronomers.) But a smaller body like Sol will only grow flatter at the poles. Its thin outer layers will be especially affected. Eventually they form a broad disc around the equator in which most of the angular momentum is concentrated, and which then breaks free. Much of this material will escape to interstellar space, but part will remain in orbit.[16] Some theorists maintain that the star does not throw off such a disc but acquires it from the nebular medium; still others have proposed that star and disc are formed together. In any event, there is coupling between them, through gravitation, magnetism, and turbulence effects.

Thus, as the disc breaks up, it remains under control of the star. A whirling agglomeration of dust, gas, and solid motes is formed. The dynamic processes that will tend to bring these particles into contact have been mathematically investigated.

Contrary to an older belief, planets form not in a molten but in a cold state. The Earth's interior grew hot only after the globe was so big that intense pressure existed and heat from radioactivity accumulated. There must be something that makes the planetesimal particles stick together on collision rather than bounce apart again or shatter. Harold C. Urey has proposed water and ammonia in a slushy state as sticking agents;[17] Hoyle suggests pitchy material resulting from the oxidation of hydrocarbons.[18] If they do not already exist in the nebula, compounds can no doubt form readily under its conditions—a comparatively dense, turbulent mass of intermingled elements, irradiated by the new star and cosmic rays, with plenty of small solid nuclei on which atoms and molecules may condense and interact still further. Of course, once a protoplanet gets big enough, it can attract and hold loose material simply by the strength of its gravitational field.

Thus we see that the planets are approximately as old as the Sun. There is even reason to think that certain light nuclei were formed in quantity on the surface of the inner planets by Solar particles bombarding heavier atoms.[19] All modern theories strongly imply that stars of the ordinary sort will acquire planets in the regular course of their development.

This is strikingly confirmed by the fact that members of the main sequence brighter than Class F5 rotate much more rapidly than those occurring later in the series. There is a sharp discontinuity at this point.[20] Where has the angular momentum of the later ones gone if not into planets? Thus it appears that suns classed as F5 through G, K, and M are attended by worlds comparable to those of our Solar System. And these main-sequence dwarfs dominate the stellar population.

But we must make certain qualifications. Unless, as some think, most of the higher elements were formed near the start of galactic history, the very old stars cannot have planets. Nothing was present in their youth but hydrogen, a little helium, and a negligible amount of other substances. At best they may be accompanied by gas giants, masses too small to shine but too big to dissipate. To be sure, there might be cases where enough higher atoms were made available in a great enough concentration—say, by a local supernova—to allow planets at a freakishly early date.

Double, triple, and other multiple stars are also considered unlikely candidates by most astronomers. It is not known whether anything smaller than a supergiant world can form independently in a medium perturbed by two or more stellar masses. If an Earth-like body did appear, its orbit would usually be unstable for the same reason, perturbation. Unless it was rather near one member of a widely separated binary, or moved at a great distance about both members of a close pair, it would be a short-lived world, doomed to fall into one or the other sun before very many millions of years had passed.[21] (In Chapter 4 I will suggest a more optimistic idea, but matters are complicated enough already in the present section.)

Nevertheless, multiple stars have furnished us another bit of evidence of other planetary families. Telescopic search is almost out of the question. If Alpha Centauri A, the brightest member of that triple system that is our nearest neighbor, and very Sun-like itself, had a planet the size and distance of Jupiter, that world would lie at the limit of detectability on long-exposure photographs taken through the two-hundred-inch Hale telescope.[22] Perhaps a large instrument on the airless Moon, together with advanced photomultiplier devices, may one day correct this situation. But all in all it seems doubtful that direct observation will ever find extra-Solar planets. Certainly such methods will never work on any but the closest suns.

The evidence comes more subtly through mathematical analysis of stellar motions. The double star 61 Cygni has been shown to possess a third component whose mass is only about sixteen times that of Jupiter. The systems 70 Ophiuchi and Lalande 21185 include similar objects, each with about ten Jovian masses. Jupiter being a full 318.3 times as heavy as Earth, one might quibble whether these are supergiant planets or sub-subdwarf stars. Since they are not big enough for thermonuclear reactions to take place at their cores, the former description looks more reasonable. In any case, they offer powerful support for the belief that most if not all stars have lesser companions, including some of Earth-like size. And there can be no question about the recently discovered object which circles Barnard's Star. Only about half again as massive as Jupiter, it is absolutely a planet; and all probability says that it cannot be very exceptional.

"Le silence éternal de ces espaces infinis m'effraie," wrote Pascal: one of the most terrifying sentences ever penned. Indeed, the thought of the chasm that reaches between the stars, the hugeness of each sun and galaxy, and the hollowness that engulfs them all, is enough to daunt the bravest spirit. But we are thinking on our own infinitesimal scale. In universal time, space is neither empty nor still. Rather, it blazes with light, seethes with the fury of supernovae and cosmic rays, roils with dust and gas, travails with new suns and new worlds—one gigantic violent splendor. In this single galaxy, at a conservative guess, there may be fifty billion planetary systems, and quite likely there are more.

Of course, to man, those globes that bear life—and especially sentience—are much the most interesting. There would be small joy in contemplating a universe where the living Earth was a mere accident, the only one of its kind. We feel instinctively that this is so grotesque as to be impossible. But only facts and careful reasoning on the basis of those facts can lead us toward the truth. To see what the likelihood is that life exists elsewhere, we must examine the origins of the only life we know so far.

Chapter 2

Life on Earth

LONG AFTER MEN had agreed that the farthest reaches of space are governed by laws that can be understood, one aspect of the world continued to escape their logic. This aspect was life. Scientists could investigate the chemistry of plants and animals. They could make important discoveries, such as the fact that it is based on the one element carbon. But there was no way to reproduce in the laboratory those incredibly complex reactions that the humblest leaf or worm controls during every second of its existence. Small wonder that they spoke of "organic chemistry" as a discipline quite alien to the study of inorganic matter. Some of the most profound workers were convinced that there must be a special quality to life, a vital force, that would forever defy measurement and cold reason.

This metaphysics received its deathblow in 1828. That was the year when Friedrich Wöhler synthesized urea, a typical biological product, from inanimate materials. Vitalism dies hard; an occasional gasp is still heard from it. But no serious thinker now believes that life is a separate kingdom within the universe. The same laws that prevail in the atom and the molecule must command the cell, the animal, and the brain. "Organic chemistry" has come to mean simply the chemistry of carbon and its compounds. Few of us today find this kinship with the stars anything but exhilarating.

Nevertheless, the difficulty in accounting for the fact of life remained. How could raw matter have developed that intricacy which even the most primitive organism must possess? Could a jumble of ordinary substances, drifting about in the air or the oceans, have collided and adhered until the first cell was formed by sheer chance? No. The odds against it are so great that the entire universe will hardly endure long enough for this to happen. Not even a protein molecule could take shape in this way.

Panspermy

Early in the twentieth century S. A. Arrhenius proposed that life had perhaps not originated here at all. The first cells might have come from outer space.

A microorganism, a bacterium for example, can easily be carried into the upper atmosphere. At that height, electrical discharges will furnish enough energy to expel the tiny thing, raising it so far that the pressure of the Sun's light sweeps it away from Earth. Light does exert pressure, minute but sufficient to propel a microbe of a certain size. And many microbes not only have such sizes but are so hardy that they can withstand the cold and vacuum of space. They assume the form of spores, a dormant state in which they can last indefinitely.

Pushed outward by the Sun, whose gravitational pull weakens with distance in exact proportion to the intensity of its light, a spore can reach the orbit of Mars in weeks, leave the Solar System in years, and drift to the nearest star in some tens of thousands of years. It can even cross the galaxy in a few hundred million years. Approaching another star, it may well become attached to a particle of cosmic dust, so big that gravitation again gets the upper hand. Thus it drifts inward, and is eventually captured by a planet. However, light pressure will continue to have some effect, slowing the speed of this fall. Being small, the spore will not burn up in the atmosphere as a meteorite does. It will gently descend—and if the planet happens to be a new one, still empty but with oceans, a potential home for life, the spore can become active again, divide, redivide, mutate, adapt, and people the world with its descendants.

Arrhenius' suggestion was attractive. Admittedly, it did not explain how the first cells had originated. But given many planets in the universe, the chance origin of life became a little more probable. The event only had to happen once. A single fertile world could seed the galaxy.

But the idea is in trouble as soon as we calculate how many

spores that planet would have to put out. As a matter of fact, if there are a hundred billion planets in the galaxy, each must eject about a ton of microbes per billion years for Earth to have a reasonable chance of picking up one individual during the first billion years of its own existence.[1] This may not be impossible. But the converse figure—the amount of microbes a single world must eject if it is the only source—is not within the bounds of reason.

Furthermore, any spores that Earth might receive (or send out) will never wake up on arrival. The Sun's ultraviolet radiation alone will kill them before they even reach Mars. X rays and cosmic rays pose a similar hazard for any hypothetical bug that can tolerate the ultraviolet.

Panspermy, as this concept is called, cannot be ruled out altogether. A spore that started far enough from the Sun, or that did not drift too far inward, would not get a lethal dose of radiation. Thus we *may* find signs of life that began outside the Solar System when we explore the moons of the big outer planets.

Such microbes, if they are there at all, cannot have come from just anywhere. The cooler stars do not exert enough light pressure, in proportion to their gravitation, to be donors; though of course they can accept spores that approach. The very hot stars are too short-lived for life as we understand it to have developed around them. Besides, as we have seen, they probably do not have planets anyway. Carl Sagan finds that the only possible donor suns lie on the main sequence, from A0 to G5.[2] The possibility of panspermy is further reduced by the likelihood that planets do not accompany stars brighter than F5.

So this process as Arrhenius described it is a very minor phenomenon in the universe, if it takes place at all. And it certainly does not involve Earth. We shall see in Chapter 3 that a variation of the idea—spores carried inside meteorites—may prove to be correct within the Solar System if not the whole galaxy. But we cannot use this to explain our own genesis.

Fortunately, there is no longer any need to do so. We have no reason to doubt that life did arise by itself on this one planet. Though its origin is not yet fully understood, it has been more than outlined. In fact, today we do not lack a theory of biopoesis, as J. D. Bernal has named the process of life's origin.[3] Rather, we have an almost embarrassing variety of theories.

Because of this, and because the subject is highly technical, it is hard to offer a coherent account within a single chapter of what is now being thought and discovered. I can only pass over the surface, pausing at a few highlights, barely hinting at some of the controversies. But then our purpose is merely to see how life is, indeed, a natural phenomenon and to lay a foundation for our later musings about its cosmic destiny.

The Environment

So we begin with the newly born Earth some four and a half billion years ago. Though the dust and stones and asteroids that formed the globe had been cold, its temperature now mounted. There were several reasons for this. Simply by falling toward each other, the original bodies lost a good deal of energy, which for the most part became heat. Internal adjustments, such as a possible slow movement of iron down toward the core, may also have released energy on a comparable scale. Finally, radioactive elements were disintegrating and warming up their surroundings. They had done this ever since they were created, of course. But the planet was much less able than the meteorites and dust particles to radiate heat.

This was due to the so-called square-cube law. Imagine that we double the radius of a sphere. Its area increases as the square of the radius, that is, it is quadrupled. But the volume is proportional to the cube of the radius, and so is multiplied by 8. Therefore the sphere has only one-half as many square inches of surface per cubic inch of volume as it did before it swelled ($4/8 = ½$). In general, if the linear dimensions of an object are increased n times, where n can be any number, the ratio of surface to volume shrinks by the factor $1/n$. We shall meet this law a number of times in many different applications.

Since heat is generated throughout the volume of a planet but can only be lost through the surface, Earth could not cool off as fast as a smaller body. So warmth accumulated and the temperature rose. It may have risen enough to melt the entire globe; or perhaps just the crust; or maybe only small regions where conditions were especially violent. No one is certain on this point. But we can be sure that for millions upon millions of years Earth was a fearsome, shuddering, flame-spurting Tartarus.

It was probably airless, too. Hydrogen and helium, the most abundant elements, are also the lightest, too light for a small planet with a weak gravitational pull to hold down. If Earth ever had an atmosphere similar to that which Jupiter and the other giant worlds still possess, it was soon lost.

However, a secondary atmosphere was generated. Water had been trapped in the body of the planet, in hydrated minerals and primordial ice. Now heat released it and drove it upward, through geysers, volcanoes, and springs. Similarly, the breakdown of carbonates yielded great quantities of carbon monoxide and dioxide. Gases such as methane (a compound of carbon and hydrogen), ammonia (a compound of nitrogen and hydrogen), and hydrogen sulfide also appeared. Too heavy to escape, these substances accumulated until Earth had a dense air envelope.

Chemical and physical processes went on within this atmosphere. Surface rocks took up carbon dioxide by forming new carbonates. Much of the gas, though, remained free, or was dissolved in the waters. Other molecules such as water itself, rising high into the air, were broken down by the strong ultraviolet radiation of the Sun. Most of the hydrogen atoms released by this breakdown disappeared into space while heavier components like oxygen were retained. But according to the majority opinion of specialists, this is not how we got the free oxygen we now have. The element is viciously reactive; it soon bound itself to other materials. Surface iron was turned to rust. Methane was oxidized through a series of reactions that released intermediate substances in small amounts, for example, organic acids. Ammonia underwent a similar fate.

Thus, by about four billion years ago, there was an atmosphere containing great quantities of nitrogen and methane; less but still respectable amounts of water vapor and ammonia; and a small but significant percentage of other substances. Because sunlight was continually attacking its compounds, these latter "impurities" included some free hydrogen, as well as carbon dioxide and hydrogen sulfide.

There were also oceans. According to W. W. Rubey, they amounted to 10 per cent or less of their present volume.[4] Chlorides, phosphates, and other salts were nonetheless dissolved in them. The land was rock, sand, and dust, often brilliantly colored by minerals, but utterly barren. Such a desert must have been hot by day and cold by night, yet the swings of temperature were not anywhere near as extreme as those we now observe on the Moon.

The reason lies in the "greenhouse effect," which we will also meet again. Once internal heat has been largely dissipated, practically all the warmth of any planet is due to the Sun's radiation. The solid body absorbs this and sends it back in all directions. But being cooler than a star, the planet radiates at longer wave lengths. Now, certain gases, notably carbon dioxide and water vapor, are opaque to a large part of these infrared waves. Hence they absorb the energy, preventing the solid ground from giving it back to space. Eventually a balance is struck, with the planet returning as much heat as it receives. But a certain heat reserve remains trapped by the atmosphere, so to speak. This keeps the surface warmer than it would have been without its gaseous blanket. In other words, carbon dioxide and water vapor act like the glass in a greenhouse, which permits sunlight to enter freely but lets heat go out only slowly. At the same time, by reflecting or absorbing much of the incoming energy itself, an atmosphere protects the surface from a very rapid rise of temperature. (The entire situation is more complicated than this and not yet perfectly understood.)

Nevertheless, temperature changes must have helped breed huge thunderstorms on the ancient Earth; and vulcanism may well have been more intense—hundreds of Krakataus erupting per century, millions of geysers and hot springs. We are sure the world lay under a cruel blast of ultraviolet light from the Sun. Today most of this powerful radiation is blocked out. Oxygen in the high atmosphere is converted to ozone by ultraviolet light, and ozone is opaque to those wave lengths. Thus only a very small amount ever reaches the surface. But in the distant past there was no free oxygen to speak of, and a man stepping out unprotected into that environment would soon have died from radiation.

And yet, in all probability, these grim conditions were what created life.

Prebiological Chemistry

Simple compounds like methane, which we know must have been present—they have been detected in the atmospheres of the giant planets and even in comets—could never give rise to a living cell. Somehow, more complex materials had to be formed. But how?

Perhaps a start was made in the Solar nebula before the worlds had coalesced. We have seen that the dust particles and actinic light must have provided good conditions for chemical reactions to take place. Complex hydrocarbons may well have formed, and conceivably some ring-shaped molecules. To be sure, if Earth passed through a molten stage, these must all have been destroyed; but Earth may not have done so. In that event, the oceans four billions years ago contained many elaborate organic substances ready-made.

Yet we do not have to believe this. In a series of experiments rightly regarded as classic, S. L. Miller in 1952 took a mixture of methane, ammonia, hydrogen, and water—stuffs that we can be sure were in the ancient atmosphere and seas—and circulated it for a week past a gentle electric discharge, which was equivalent in its effect to ultraviolet radiation. Analyzing the colored material that resulted, he found certain amino acids.[5]

Now these are among the substances basic to Terrestrial life. Amino acids, compounds of carbon, hydrogen, oxygen, and nitrogen, are the building blocks of proteins. And proteins, in turn, are the versatile materials out of whose near-infinite variety much of every living organism is made, from the shell of a tobacco mosaic virus to the muscles of a human body. The enzymes, organic catalysts, which govern the intricate chemistry of life—and without which many essential reactions

Other experimenters have subsequently produced amino acids in other ways, for example, by exposing formaldehyde and nitrate to the action of sunlight.[6] Other biologically essential materials, such as sugars, lipids, purines, pyrroles, and pyrimidines have also been created, or will soon be created, in ongoing experiments which employ similarly simple agents. For instance, purines have been formed in the laboratory by polymerizing—linking together—molecules of hydrogen cyanide, which doubtless was present to some extent on the ancient world.[7] In general, organic molecules, activated by radiation, lightning, or other strong energy sources, have a powerful tendency to interact, forming more complex substances. There is no longer any doubt that nature created these compounds—some of them, at least—before there was life on Earth.

Some workers have objected that the very ultraviolet light that gave rise to those compounds would break them down again. This is true—but only where there was no protection. Molecules formed close to the water, and sinking down under the surface, would be amply shielded. Furthermore, the oxygenless atmosphere was not completely transparent to all radiations. Some were absorbed; especially, as it happens, those wave lengths most destructive to organic substances. Thus a big molecule formed in the upper atmosphere, descending toward the ground before it chanced to absorb a quantum of ultraviolet energy, would also be safe.[8]

This evolution of matter could not happen today. Not only does oxygen destroy many organic compounds in short order, but others would rapidly be devoured by microbes. In the past, however, there was no free oxygen and no life. Nothing prevented organic material from accumulating.

In the course of time, very high concentrations were built up. The ocean must have dissolved immense quantities. A fairly old concept is that this went on until it became what has been picturesquely described as a thin warm soup. The idea is easy to credit when we recall that the seas were less extensive then than now. Even greater concentrations could have built up in limited areas. One thinks of lagoons, pools, lakes, and marshes; they may have become thick soups!

The development of prebiological compounds seems to have occurred faster than was once believed. There is good geological reason to think that free oxygen appeared more than three and a half billion years ago. Since most if not all authorities believe that this gas was released by plant cells, it follows that they came rather early in Earth's history.[9] When we consider the chemical situation, we begin to understand why this should be. The stronger a solution is, the better the chance of molecules within it to bump into other molecules with which they can react. When very many assorted reactions are going on, consecutively and successively, even the most complicated and unlikely substances seem sure to be formed.

This line of reasoning gets paradoxical support from some recent criticisms of the hypothesis that organic matter simply accumulated in the seas. Such compounds are not only broken down by radiation, they can also disintegrate spontaneously, so they do not pile up in indefinitely large amounts. If heavy hydrocarbons were formed in quantity, they must have settled to the ocean floor and been changed to graphite when the mud hardened into rock. But the fact of the matter is that very old (Pre-Cambrian) deposits have no more graphite in them than do younger ones. The seas must have been considerably more alkaline under ancient conditions, and such an environment is hostile to carbohydrates. If fats appeared at all, which is unlikely, they would react with ions such as magnesium to form hard insoluble soaps. Many other compounds would react with each other to form nonbiological compounds.[10]

Objections such as these do not disprove the general principle we have been discussing, but they do indicate that its application was more intricate, and probably more rapid, than the soup theory maintains. Doubtless much organic matter was dissolved in the oceans; but the most complex materials may have formed under more special conditions. For instance, Bernal has pointed out that molecules tend to cluster on the finely divided particles in clay soils and quartz sands. This produces concentrations higher than simple water solutions can ever become.[11]

Protocells

A. I. Oparin has developed a quite detailed theory, which is too technical for me to do more than sketch here. An extremely small particle, though larger than a molecule, that maintains its identity is known as a colloid. Fog, a colloidal suspension of water in air, is a familiar example. Such particles readily acquire an electric charge—whether positive or negative depends on the substance involved—and in water, which is a poor conductor of electricity, they retain this charge. Hence they repel each other and so do not coagulate. But if some salt is added to the water, making it a good conductor, the charge is lost and the colloids come together and precipitate. Adding a colloid with an opposite charge will also bring about this result.

Now, certain materials, including proteins, have a strong tendency in water to form a type of colloid known as a coacervate. This consists of very small, highly concentrated drops that are remarkably stable and hard to coagulate. The best explanation for the stability is that the coacervate material has so strong an affinity for the water molecule that each droplet is protected by a virtual skin of water. Nevertheless, coacervates are not inert. Indeed, they behave remarkably like living cells, being able to grow by absorbing different dissolved substances from the surrounding medium. Thus they produce intensely concentrated solutions—with all that this implies—and offer a sheltered environment where elaborate structures can develop.[12]

There is no doubt that given amino acids in the correct proportions with the right physical conditions, proteins will form. Such experiments have been carried out in the laboratory. By taking mixtures of amino acids and dissolved minerals that we can reasonably suppose were present in the ancient waters, and by heating them to temperatures that hot-springs regions could easily have supplied, Sidney W. Fox and his co-workers have obtained materials that they call proteinoids. They are the result of amino acid units joining together, and are as large and complex as natural proteins.

The proteinoids have a number of remarkable properties. Not least is their ability under simple treatment (for example, adding hot water and then allowing the solution to cool) to form spherules. These little balls are about the size of bacteria, and quite stable, but they behave in an even more lifelike way than coacervates.[13] Under various conditions—all geologically reasonable—they will form skinlike outer boundaries, twin, and join into chains.[14]

Indeed, so readily do these tiny, intricate structures form that Fox suggests the microfossils found in very old coal beds may not be of biological origin at all.[15] At the same time, his observations go far to bear out the idea that when the conditions were right, life developed naturally and rapidly.

This in turn indicates how widespread life must be throughout the universe. Of course, extra-Terrestrial life does not have to be identical with ours. In fact, the chances are that no two planets have biological systems precisely alike, no matter how similar the worlds may be physically. The degree of possible difference is still debatable. Accident may often have decided which pathway our prebiological and early biological evolution took. The proteinoid spherules, for instance, show a variety of structure, behavior, and chemical composition. However, many workers, including Fox, feel that the sequence of phenomena shows much internal direction rather than randomness. Certainly natural law must impose some limits on the possibilities. We are not yet quite certain how wide or narrow those limits are.

An interesting problem in this connection is that of isomerism. Most organic molecules can occur in more than one form (isomer), distinguished by the way the atoms are arranged. Two such arrangements that are mirror images of each other are called optical antipodes because they have opposite effects on polarized light passing through solutions of them. One antipode rotates the plane of polarization (the plane in which the light waves vibrate) to the right, and is therefore called the *dextro-* or *d*-configuration. The other antipode rotates the plane of polarization to the left and so is called the *levo-* or *l*-configuration.

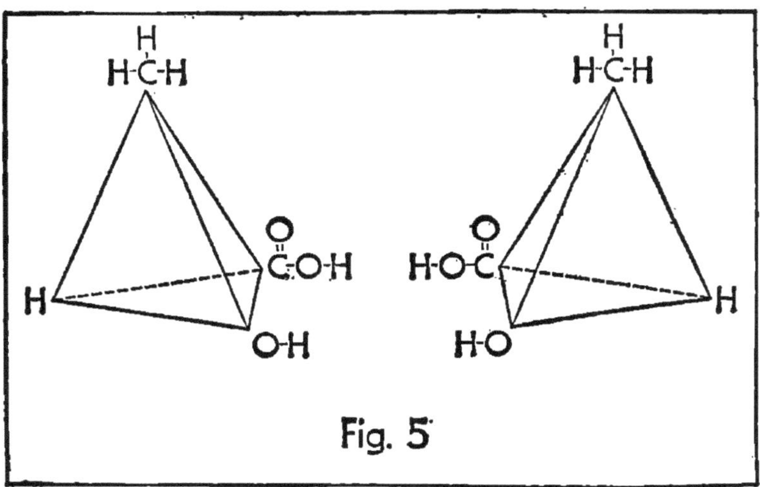

Fig. 5

Fig. 5 shows, in a simplified form, the two varieties of lactic acid. Each letter stands for an atom: *C* for carbon, *O* for oxygen, *H* for hydrogen. (The central carbon atom, to which the other four groups are attached, is not shown, and only the very short lines within those groups represent chemical bonds.) The molecule is pyramid-shaped, and the reader can easily see how each isomer is a mirror image of the other.

Now, in experiments like Miller's, equal quantities of *d*- and *l*-amino acids appeared. But in living nature, almost without exception, all these materials are of the *l*-configuration. (Only a few bacteria and fungi produce *d*-amino acids.) As a general rule, all those organic molecules important to life occur in only one isomer when manufactured by a living organism, whereas man's laboratory work produces both forms impartially.

It is not hard to understand why life should do this. Once such a tendency gets built in, so to speak, it is self-perpetuating. An automated factory programed to weave percale does not suddenly begin making denim. But we may ask why it is turning out percale in the first place. Similarly, we may ask why life is turning out one form of molecule when the other form must have been equally available in the beginning. There is no reason to think one mirror image is inherently superior to the other.

Some theorists have suggested that Earth's magnetic field or the polarization of ultraviolet light by the atmosphere may somehow be responsible. If this is true, then we can guess that our kind of isomers dominate the universe. But there is no real reason to believe it is true. We can imagine ways in which sheer accident can have made the choice for us back in that age when the shadowy borderline between life and nonlife was crossed.

Let us consider the process in a little more detail. To begin with the commonest theory of biopoesis, remember what incessant random interaction was going on in oceans and atmosphere, clays and sands, coacervates and proteinoid spherules —all these sites have been suggested, and perhaps all the suggestions are correct. We must use that word "random" carefully. Two molecules, colliding, do not hook up in any old way. The laws of nature limit the possibilities and thus give a general direction to this blind chemical evolution. However, the more complex the interacting molecules are, the wider the range of possibilities. So eventually, in the far past, there occurred the production of substances known as nucleoproteins. Certain members of this class had life's ability to reproduce itself.

Not that there is any question of a "vital spark" bestowed at this time. The self-replication of nucleoprotein is a purely chemical matter and fairly well understood. As such a molecule encounters suitable simpler molecules, its configuration of atoms and electric charges forces the latter to line up and combine with each other according to its own pattern. Many inorganic crystals, dropped into a strong solution of their own substance, do the same thing in a less elaborate fashion. Nonetheless, this self-replication—this ability to make *foreign* materials into a copy of oneself—is a fundamental characteristic of life.

(For the sake of accuracy, I should add that the self-replication work is actually done by nucleic acid, which is one component of nucleoprotein. Accordingly, many thinkers believe the first biological molecule was simply a nucleic acid. But since this is less stable than a protein, it seems more likely to have come into being as part of a larger and sturdier molecule. Only afterward, in the protected environment of a cell, did the nucleic acids isolate themselves and build chromosomes.)

Evidently the first successful nucleoprotein happened to contain only *l*-amino acids. This is not as improbable as one would think. Self-replication should be much easier for a homogeneous than a heterogeneous molecule. Indeed, the latter may be incapable of this feat. If so, the chances of getting all *l*-aminos or all *d*-aminos become fifty-fifty. Whichever kind happened to be formed first would take over the world in an explosive spread through the oceans.

Not all authorities accept the "naked molecule" concept of life's origins. Oparin, in particular, argues that entire systems evolved. Coacervates, absorbing materials from the water, provided an environment in which networks of interaction took place. Catalysts were formed, promoting specific reactions. Gradually these different catalytic agents became more and more co-ordinated. The system organized itself spatially as well as chemically, developing an internal structure that localized particular processes at the most useful sites. In other words, rather than beginning with a molecular system that slowly acquired extra parts, theories like Oparin's begin with a colloidal protocell that slowly developed interior complexity. To be sure, the vast majority of these protocells must have been self-destroying failures. But evolution only needed one, perhaps, that became able to reproduce itself.[16]

Photosynthesis

Large molecule, viruslike molecular aggregate, or crude protocell—whatever it was—the first living thing multiplied until its descendants filled the oceans. The rich stock of organic nutrients, which had accumulated for so many millions of years, was soon exhausted. Life could expand no further, and must indeed have come close to perishing. Bernal even suggests that it may have arisen and committed suicide a number of times in precisely this way.[17] More likely, though, it simply stopped reproducing. Nature continued to make organic matter, but very few proto-organisms were lucky enough to find these molecules. The rest, dormant, suffered gradual attrition. Heat, radiation, and mutation destroyed them.

The mutation rate (the rate at which the heredity itself changes) must have been very high. The heredity-bearing molecules of that time were more exposed than today's genes, which not only are surrounded by their cell but are also furnished a protective enzyme. Furthermore, the ancient nucleoproteins or nucleic acids must have been smaller and simpler than the modern ones, hence more profoundly affected by any random change in some part of themselves. Therefore, heat, radiation, and chance chemical encounters mutated the early life forms at a tremendous rate. Higher forms of life could not have survived these conditions, and no doubt untold primitive forms perished. But being so simple and unspecialized, others got along, even when drastically altered. (Mutation of a single-celled organism obviously affects the organism itself as well as its descendants.) And—once in a great while—such a change was beneficial.

One improvement in these lean millenniums may well have been the ability to get food actively, instead of absorbing it passively from the water. That is, some primitive cells "learned" how to engulf and digest other organisms. We do not know whether the first microscopic hunters evolved at just this time, earlier, or later. But if it was in the age of scarcity, we can easily imagine how the new type of cell triumphantly swept the planet, devouring all else—and found itself back in the same blind alley of no food supply.

But then evolution took a third fundamental step. The first had been the development of complex molecules and aggregates, the second the development of cells with interior metabolism and the ability to reproduce. The third was photosynthesis. Some cells became able to make their own food. With the help of the substance chlorophyll, they used sunlight to energize a reaction between carbon dioxide and water. This produced sugar, which the cells converted into other needed materials.* The development of these microbial plants doubtless took place by stages rather than all at once, but each generation was increasingly less dependent on the outside world for its food. Once again life multiplied explosively. And this time it did not starve afterward.

As everyone knows, free oxygen is released in the course of photosynthesis. The one-celled plants, swarming in the waters, poured immense quantities of this gas into the atmosphere, utterly changing its character. I have already mentioned how powerfully reactive oxygen is. The early organic and nitrogenous gases—methane, ammonia, and their derivatives—were oxidized. Carbon dioxide, water, and free nitrogen replaced them. The first two went to promote the growth of more plant cells; the last remained loose until it made up three-fourths of the air. Meanwhile, an ozone layer formed high up, shutting off most of the Sun's ultraviolet rays. This may have killed some species of cells that had come to require those wave lengths; but others adapted, or were positively benefited. The oxygen itself posed a graver threat and probably destroyed many early life forms, including plants. But others developed chemical and physical defenses. To this day, oxygen poisons cell nuclei if they are directly exposed to it.

In time some varieties of cells even began to make use of this gas. By causing oxygen to react with molecules they had assimilated elsewhere, they derived energy by which to move, grow, and reproduce. What was the source of those molecules? Other cells, including, more and more, the plants. In this way arose the separation between animal and vegetable kingdoms. This division is not absolute. Not only are there borderline cases, but chemistry itself bears the mark of their common ancestry. For instance, chlorophyll is closely related to hemoglobin, the material that carries oxygen in the blood of most animals. The chief difference is that chlorophyll has an atom of magnesium at the place where hemoglobin has an atom of iron.

* Recent evidence indicates that amino acids and perhaps other compounds are also formed directly by photosynthesis rather than by a later process.

Generalization

We can leave the genesis of life at this point, for the rest of the evolutionary story is familiar enough. Not that we know in any detail how multicelled organisms developed, and the land was conquered, and intelligence arose. But we feel confident that given well-developed one-celled life, all these other things can happen and eventually will happen. And after considering all the evidence, we feel equally confident that given the right kind of planet, the evolution of the original cells also can and will happen.

But we are still not sure what the right kind of planet is. Obviously Earth-like worlds are suitable. But might other initial environments also serve? What are the really basic requirements of biopoesis?

Apparently there are three. First, a reasonably abundant supply of molecules that are potentially able to form more complex substances. Second, an energy source that will activate the simple molecules. Third, a solvent in which materials can be concentrated and reactions can easily take place.

On Earth the first requirement was met by methane, ammonia, and other simple substances, including such inorganic materials as the phosphates. These must be widely available on the smaller planets of the universe and maybe on the giant ones.

The second requirement was met by ultraviolet light, heat, lightning, perhaps radioactivity, or even acoustic phenomena.[18] It is hard to imagine how equivalent energy can be found on ultracold worlds like Neptune or Pluto. We may concede the possibility of a very slow evolution toward life under low-temperature conditions, but only if a solvent is there.

This third requirement was met by water on Earth, and met admirably. Not any substance that happens to be liquid under the planet's conditions will serve. Various chemical and electrical properties are also necessary, or the solvent will not be versatile enough. Certain physical properties are also desirable —for example, the high specific heat of water helps protect delicate biological mechanisms from unduly swift temperature changes—and they may be essential.

Liquid ammonia seems to fit the specifications rather well. It is the only really plausible alternative to water, though I shall discuss some other possibilities later. In all events, if a solvent exists, it cannot dissolve anything when the temperature is so high that it is a gas or so low that it is a solid. This may set limits to the range within which life can evolve—or it may not. Before speculating, let us see what facts we possess about other worlds.

In this Solar System we know nine planets and a great many lesser bodies. We are standing on one. What is the chance that all the rest are empty and that we are alone beneath our star?

Chapter 3

Sisters Under the Sun

KNOWLEDGE does not advance in a single wave, spreading outward from the realm of things about which we can be sure into a boundless unknown. Rather, we make the easy discoveries first, however unrelated they are to each other. Only afterward do we investigate the harder, less obvious fields and the connections between. But what we then learn is apt to change our views of those areas that were first studied. They no longer look so easy to understand.

Thus, in astronomy, Newtonian mechanics gave a basic comprehension of the stars and planets, which in turn gave impetus to atomic research. But then the new concepts of nuclear physics and quantum theory revolutionized our ideas about the stars. Now biological science is being similarly transmuted. And, at belated last, so is planetary astronomy.

For a long time the study of our own Solar System, apart from the Sun, lay neglected. The feeling prevailed that everything important was known about it. Those who raised questions were generally ignored, if only because their problems looked trivial against the exciting development of stellar and galactic dynamics. A few workers continued in our local vineyard, because they loved it. And in the past decade or so they have begun to reap a bountiful harvest. Interest in the planets has revived throughout other sciences besides astronomy. This is not just because expeditions are planned. Suddenly we have realized how much we do not know about our neighbors. Since it appears that most stars have similar companions, planetary astronomy is more than a sideline. It is essential to our comprehension of the universe as a whole.

This book cannot review all the new riddles or even many of the tentative answers. Instead it will focus on one aspect, the planets as homes for living organisms. Most books admit the possibility of low plant forms or lichens on Mars. Some will add that Venus may also harbor life, but we know too little about its surface conditions to make any safe guesses. The rest of the Solar System is shrugged off: too hot, too cold, airless or waterless or both. But the problem is much more complex than that.

Meteoritic Evidence

So far, the only actual, weighable stuff that we have from space consists of meteorites. These lumps of stone or nickel-iron do not offhand seem likely carriers for traces of life "out there." Have they not always been mere boulders, orbiting in vacuum, seared by the Sun's actinic light and by cosmic rays? Would not their fiery passage through Earth's atmosphere destroy whatever organic material might somehow have existed in them?

The answer to the second question is a flat No. Although the surface of a meteorite is sterilized by its fall, the time is too short for the interior to heat up much. A germ on the inside would not suffer harm. However, Earth is so wealthy in microscopic life that it is hard indeed to make sure that anything found on opening a meteorite is not simply due to local contamination. As long ago as 1895 such experiments were made, and discounted for just this reason.

Recently, under still more elaborate precautions, the investigation has been repeated. Some bacteria were found and cultured, with unusual difficulty; to date they have not been identified. The modern workers do not insist that these organisms are of extra-Terrestrial origin. Indeed, the consensus appears to be that they are native ones, which got in through fine pores in the mass—as we suppose any alien germs would have done—despite all safeguards.[1]

The tantalizing possibility does remain, however remote, that they are not indigenous. Though panspermy by light pressure is no longer taken seriously, scientists admit that a variation of it can occur. A shower of rocks can actually be thrown into space from an Earth-sized world—by the impact of a monstrous meteorite, a flying mountain like the ones that shaped Arizona's Meteor Crater or the Rieskessel in Germany.

Microbes, encapsulated in these lumps, would be safe from ultraviolet and most cosmic radiation. They could survive for a very long time as spores until the chances of orbital perturbation brought their vessel close enough for Earth to capture it. Similarly, our own planet must have lost microorganisms in the past.

A discovery less equivocal than bacterial cultures was made not long ago. It has to do with a class of meteorites known, from their composition, as the chondrites. Some of them, adding up to around 2 per cent of all known meteorites, are carbonaceous. That is, organic materials have been found within them, totaling about 0.5 per cent of the mass.[2] These materials are definitely not living. They are, however, saturated hydrocarbons of some complexity, such as are generally associated with biological phenomena. And they do appear to be extra-Terrestrial. No contamination process is known that could produce them inside the nutritionless, nearly sealed body of a stone.[3]

It is tempting to believe that these compounds are the remnants of germs that did not last out a space voyage, either because their meteorites were ejected too violently from the parent body or because they were too long adrift in the void. (The survival time of an encapsulated spore is not infinite. If nothing else, its own natural radioactivity and that of its meteoritic vessel will damage it. Dormant, it cannot repair this damage, which is therefore cumulative. The maximum span is thus estimated at about a million years.[4] Quite apart from all other considerations, this pretty well eliminates interstellar panspermy, though transfer of living material within the Solar System remains somewhat plausible.)

However, a more cautious explanation will fit the facts equally well. These hydrocarbons may be precursors of life, brought to being under the very conditions in space that seem to forbid any biology at all.

As we have seen, there is a possibility that organic chemicals were formed very early in the development of the Solar System, before the planets themselves. The carbonaceous chondrites may be leftovers from this ancient time. Or they may be somewhat younger, perhaps from the Moon.

Luna

This brings up the question of Lunar life. At first glance our satellite looks more sterile than an operating table. With its small diameter, 2,160 miles, and low mass, twelve-thousandths that of Earth, its escape velocity is a mere one and one-half miles per second. Thus it was unable to hold an atmosphere, which leaked into space until today no detectable amount remains. (Heavy gases like xenon may have been retained to the extent of a billionth of our own sea-level air density, but this is not certain and makes little practical difference in any event.[5]) Water vapor disappeared in the same way until the Lunar surface was bone dry. Without atmospheric insulation, without moderating seas and lakes, the desert of jagged mountains, craters, and dark plains that is the Moon swings wildly between temperature extremes. At high noon of the two-week day, the surface is over 200° F., but at midnight it drops to 250° below zero. Biologically worse is the lack of any shield against radiation. The blast of ultraviolet rays and the gales of charged particles from Solar flares would soon destroy any organism left exposed. In time the very molecules of organic material would be broken down.

But this is not the whole story. After all, though we think of this Earth as fertile, most of its solid surface is a cold still blackness where only a few creatures can live, feeding on carrion and each other—the ocean beds. The Moon is equally complex. Just because there is no atmosphere and hence no convection, anything that casts a shadow is a barrier to light and radiation. The many Lunar crevasses and caves are never subjected to the Sun's attack.

Moreover, although the American and Soviet vehicles that landed instruments on the Moon have proved that it is not entirely covered with dust as some people thought, Earth-bound observations do indicate that large areas are so insulated. Radio emissions show that temperatures a few feet below this layer vary from about +30° F. to −95° F.[6] If not actually miles deep, it may well be quite thick in places. Fred Whipple has pointed out that such a layer under irradiation in a vacuum congeals into a light semiporous material.[7] If Moon dust is similar, this matrix should offer an ideal hiding place for organic matter.

Be this as it may, the Moon probably does not have the crust-mantle-and-core structure of Earth but is a fairly uniform rocky ball. This fact, together with the low gravity, suggests that it has caverns and tunnels far more extensive than any we know here. If so, the protected Lunar environment is actually rather large.

In short, nothing forbids the Moon's having preserved a good deal of organic material. This may have come from space as part of the regular meteoritic infall—which, under conditions of airlessness, has been much heavier on the Lunar than the Terrestrial surface. If complex molecules were indeed formed under primordial conditions, we may well expect the Moon to be a repository of such scientifically priceless relics.

But as Sagan remarks, it is by no means impossible that organic material originated on the Moon itself. It must have had a primitive atmosphere similar to Earth's, which it lost in the same way, though at a faster rate. Geochemistry—or selenochemistry—must also have produced a secondary atmosphere that lasted for a while, and even bodies of water. The greenhouse effect would have moderated the temperature cycle, thus possibly slowing the rate of air loss. Conceivably the Moon had a noticeable secondary atmosphere and surface water for as long as ten million or even one hundred million years.

So conditions were once right for the evolution of protolife, and may have remained right long enough for the event to occur. Actual organisms may even have appeared. If these died when the air departed, their traces should remain under the dust. Sagan calculates that the organic matter could amount to several grams per square centimeter, and he emphasizes the importance of sterilizing all our Lunar probes. A few Terrestrial bacteria—surviving in the protected areas, consuming these substances, and multiplying—could destroy a treasure hoard of irreplacable data about the origin of life.

But might not some of the native forms have survived on their own? The Moon cannot be an utter waste. It seems very possible that much of its water remains in the form of subsurface ice. Some of this, in the course of the long Lunar day, ought to assume the liquid and vapor forms. Thus parts of the Moon would have two requirements for life: moisture and an equable temperature. Furthermore, the Lunar atmosphere was not lost overnight, especially by the standards of microorganisms with their short generations. Was there not time for them to adapt to changing conditions? Did not those kinds of life that became extinct leave a legacy of organic matter that the survivors could use? There is no known reason why the Moon *cannot* have an extensive microbial population. If so, its contamination by Terrestrial germs would be a scientific catastrophe.[8]

To be sure, some thinkers have suggested that this contamination has already occurred. Meteorites cast off from Earth may have struck the Moon with a living cargo eons ago. In that case, forms long extinct on this planet may be found up there, as tiny fossils or as adapted immigrants. They would perhaps be more vulnerable to modern germs from Earth than would strictly native Lunar species, whose biochemistry may be different from the Terrestrial. Again, we must not risk losing such an opportunity for knowledge through our own carelessness. Luckily, the hazard is not great if due precautions are taken.

No one claims that the idea of life on the Moon is anything but speculative, though the speculation has a solid factual basis. Nor has any scientist gone so far beyond the data as to suggest that such life can be anything but microscopic. And yet, our telescopes could not reveal scattered stands of cactuslike organisms. Imagine them as symbiotic communities, each member of the union performing some essential task. One grows a tough membrane to screen out undue ultraviolet light and prevent water loss. Several others in chemical series use Solar energy to metabolize local minerals for the stuff of organic synthesis. Safely buried under dust, certain nodules manufacture the enzymes needed to repair radiation damage. Reproduction is the job of wormlike or beetlelike animals that, burrowing everywhere, carry seeds to other places where conditions are favorable; in return, they get nourishment. Dying and decaying, all the symbionts furnish organic matter to the subsurface ecology.

I do not advance this idea very seriously. There are too many observations. For one thing, the Lunar atmosphere and hydrosphere were doubtless lost before any hypothetical native life had time to develop into anything but primitive one-celled organisms at best. If these adapted to conditions of airlessness, was it possible for evolution to go further? Would not the conditions at the surface and immediately below destroy whatever happened to venture there? We cannot be absolutely sure, but we can say that the existence of highly evolved Lunar forms is exceedingly improbable.

However, our look at the Moon does prove how little we know for certain and how ill we can afford to be cocksure, even when our feet are firmly planted on scientific fact. The other planets offer still more room for imagination.

Rather than recapitulate what is available elsewhere, I shall summarize the basic data in Table 1, bearing in mind that not all these figures are equally well established and authorities disagree on some of them.* Let us now consider each member of the Solar System from the standpoint of possible habitability.

Mercury

The innermost planet, Mercury, looks altogether hellish. When closest to the Sun, a bare 28.5 million miles—the orbit is highly eccentric—this tiny world receives ten times the irradiation of Earth or Luna, and the maximum temperature has been measured by thermocouple techniques as 770° F. At the geratest distance, 43.5 million miles, it is still hot enough to melt lead.

Until quite recently, it was believed that Mercury always turns the same face to the Sun, as Luna does to Earth. The other side would thus lie eternally in starlit darkness and a cold not far above absolute zero. Possibly it was covered with frozen gases, remnants of an original atmosphere which, weakly held by the low gravitation, had otherwise been dissipated by the fierce Solar bombardment.[9]

But, as very often in astronomy, the taken-for-granted idea proved quite false. When direct measurements of the night temperature were finally made, it turned out to be in

* Principal sources: Ley, Urey, and *Handbook of Chemistry and Physics.*

Name	Average Distance from Sun (A.U.)	Eccentricity of Orbit	Period of Revolution (Years)	Equatorial Diameter (Miles)	Period of Rotation (Days)	Mass (Earth = 1.00)	Average Density (Water = 1.00)	Surface Gravity (Earth = 1.00)	Escape Velocity (miles per second)
Mercury	0.39	0.20	0.23	3,100	58.4(?)	0.05	5.05	0.36	2.5
Venus	0.72	0.01	0.62	7,700	−234.16	0.81	4.88	0.86	6.3
Earth	1.00	0.02	1.00	7,900	1.00	1.00	5.52	1.00	7.0
Mars	1.52	0.09	1.88	4,200	1.02	0.11	4.24	0.40	3.1
Jupiter	5.20	0.05	11.86	88,700	0.41	318.35	1.33	2.65	37.2
Saturn	9.54	0.06	29.46	71,500	0.43	95.3	0.71	1.17	22.0
Uranus	19.19	0.05	84.02	29,500	0.45	14.54	1.56	1.09	13.8
Neptune	30.07	0.01	164.79	27,600	0.65	17.26	2.22	1.41	15.5
Pluto	39.32	0.25	248.43	3,500(?)	6.39	0.03(?)	2.0(?)	0.16(?)	1.8(?)

the neighborhood of Terrestrial room conditions, roughly 50° F. Obviously a good deal of heat is being transferred from the lighted hemisphere—so much that there has to be a fair amount of air to carry it by circulation. Next, radar studies showed that Mercury does *not* spin on its axis just once in its year. The period is about 60 Terrestrial days. In the course of this time, every part of the Mercurian surface experiences an alternation of day and night.

Explanations of these startling discoveries are being developed. With admirably keen hindsight, theory shows that Mercury's rotation period should, indeed, be just two-thirds of its revolution. The air is probably mostly hydrogen, en route from the Sun. In effect, Mercury's winds are the Solar winds. Of course, the planet may retain a few heavy gases of its own, such as a little carbon dioxide.

We thus get a picture of stark mountains, seared and cracked plains, metal pools that freeze after nightfall, thin scudding hazes, air that would be unbreathable even if it were not so tenuous, a swollen Sun and a storm of lethal radiation. Surely no life could survive, let alone arise, in this environment.

The conservative guess is that nothing lives here. But remember Luna. Mercury should also possess dust layers, protected caverns, perhaps underground glaciers, even underground water that the air keeps from boiling off. In so many square miles there must be a varied topography—including, possibly, potential bridgeheads for life. If there never was any native evolution, microbes may still have arrived by meteorite: for example, Moon specimens, which had already gone a long way toward adapting to Mercurian conditions. We cannot entirely rule out the possibility of some small functioning organisms. And these could tell us much about the fundamental laws of biology that we never suspected.

I will not now speculate about larger forms. It is hard to imagine how life as we know it could maintain even a toehold on Mercury, but I will touch on the subject again in Chapter 5, in connection with life as we do not know it, organisms that may not be dependent on one narrow range of temperature and chemical conditions.

Venus

Next out from the Sun lies Venus, most maddening of planets. As Table 1 shows, it is a near twin of Earth, a little smaller but quite able to retain a dense atmosphere, closer to the Sun but subjected to only one and nine-tenths the radiation we get. Under ideal conditions, this would make its mean absolute temperature about 20 per cent higher than ours. The equator would not be habitable except far above sea level, but the polar regions should be. However, conditions are otherwise; a few generations ago, they looked better than ideal. Venus is wrapped in a permanent cloud layer, which reflects 76 per cent of the sunlight. Down below, theorists said, it must still be warmer on the average than here—Earth is pretty reflective too—but nowhere intolerably hot. The picture was drawn of a tropical planet, overcast when the frequent rains were not falling, covered with misty jungle, swamp, and ocean, where lived animals comparable to those of our Carboniferous or Jurassic periods. Astronomers admitted there could even be creatures that had developed sentience; though since they never saw the sky and thus had no astronomy, they must be savages. Man could walk about freely on Venus when one day his spaceships landed. In the cooler, drier highlands he might colonize whole new Americas.

The image was attractive and colorful. Unfortunately, research continued and more was learned.

One reason for the effort was to discover the rotation period of Venus. With any surface markings hidden by clouds, this could not obtained by just looking. But lately radar results indicate that the Cytherean* day is about 243 times as long as the Terrestrial. And the planet rotates in a direction—east-to-west—opposite to that of all the others. The reason for this strange behavior is uncertain. Perhaps Solar tides, acting on the dense atmosphere, gradually produced it.

Spectroscopy failed to locate oxygen or water vapor but did show that the atmosphere holds large amounts of carbon

* The common adjective "Venusian" is a barbarism, and "Venereal" or "Venerean" have unhappy connotations, so "Cyntherean" is preferred by many astronomers.

dioxide—though doubtless its main constituent is nitrogen, as is the case for Earth. A man could not breathe on Venus without an air helmet. Even the lowest estimated concentration of carbon dioxide is enough to kill him. Furthermore, this gas is important to the greenhouse effect. Venus' temperature must lie well above what would be expected from Solar radiation alone. The idea therefore developed that the planet is one gigantic desert, where dust and sand are blown on hurricanes whose temperature hovers around 200° F. The clouds were variously described as dust, as powdered salts from the beds of dried-up oceans, as smoglike droplets of primordial petroleum, or as polymers of an organic compound like formaldehyde.

Of course, all we can see from a distance is the upper surface of the cloud layer. We do not observe anything that lies below. It was pointed out that at such an elevation water vapor may be frozen and hence undetectable. The clouds may be similar to those of Earth after all, though higher and denser. Urey has shown that large amounts of carbon dioxide cannot persist if there is also water in a liquid state, for then the gas reacts with silicate rocks to form carbonates. But perhaps there are no surface rocks. Venus might be covered by water, with little or no land. Bearing in mind how much carbonic acid must be dissolved there, someone has facetiously described this as an ocean of club soda.

Recent observations made by automatic equipment suspended from balloons that got above the worst interference of our own atmosphere have apparently shown that water vapor does exist in detectable amounts above the clouds. In that event, the totally dry Venus must be forgotten. But other data are less encouraging. Radio studies indicate a temperature of over 800° F. This may prove to be in an upper layer of air, with the surface cooler. But it seems unlikely. The chances are that Cytherean ground temperatures are comparable to those of Mercury's bright side.

On this basis, Sagan proposes that the planet is indeed arid, not because there is no water at all, but because whatever water there is has all vaporized and risen to form the clouds. In this situation, Urey's weathering process does not take place. Erosion must chiefly be by wind and thermal effects. Although furnace hot, the winds are gentle, since most of the Sun's energy goes into warming a dense air mass whose ground-level pressure is ten or more times that of Earth. The Cytherean atmosphere seems to be approximately 5 per cent carbon dioxide and 95 per cent nitrogen, with some chemical impurities.[10] These include carbon compounds, which lend the clouds their yellowish color. There must also be a slight trace of oxygen, because its compounds are broken down by Solar radiation —but not enough to do men any good.[11]

The reason why Earth's sister evolved in so dismal a fashion is obscure. Both planets must have exuded similar amounts of water and carbon dioxide. But Earth's share of carbon dioxide became largely fixed in rocks while Venus' remained free. Perhaps—a guess of my own—continents were never raised to any significant extent above the sea that may have existed on Venus. This in turn might be blamed on the planet's mass, somewhat less than Earth's, not squeezing the core hard enough to start orogenic processes. Whatever the cause, the carbon dioxide produced a greenhouse effect, which raised the temperature until water boiled; and this vapor is likewise a good retainer of heat. Sagan does not think that extensive bodies of water could have lasted very long.

Thus it seems most unlikely that any life ever appeared on Venus or that any meteoritic newcomers survived. We cannot be absolutely sure there is no microbial ecology below the surface or high in the atmosphere, but the chances look slim indeed.

And yet, paradoxically, this inferno may have the potential of becoming the life-richest member of the Solar System. Of course, we do not know whether Venus could be artificially seeded, and in all events any such project must wait until the planet has been thoroughly studied in its present unique condition.

But as Sagan reminds us,[12] the blue-green algae of the Nostocaceae family can live at elevated temperatures, fixing atmospheric nitrogen and evolving oxygen by photosynthesis. Planted in the upper Cytherean air, among the clouds, and supplied with any trace minerals that may be necessary (if nature does not do this via cosmic dust particles and other micrometeorites), such organisms may be able to live and reproduce. In fact, with no natural enemies, they might even multiply explosively, filling their environment almost overnight. At the appropriate altitude, then, they will convert carbon dioxide and water vapor to complex organic compounds and free oxygen. Carried by air currents down to hotter levels, the organisms will be roasted and, in the ideal case, decompose to elementary carbon and water. Thus the water is a catalyst by which carbon dioxide is broken down.

As the composition of the atmosphere changes, the greenhouse effect will weaken until temperatures drop below the boiling point of water. Then photosynthesis can proceed on the surface. Eventually the planet will be so cool that rain can fall—a tremendous Noachian rain. The Urey equilibrium will come into play, raw rock consuming still more carbon dioxide; higher forms of plant life can be introduced, and also, in due course, animals and men.

I need hardly repeat Sagan's warning of how imaginative this idea is at the present stage of things. Yet nothing in the basic laws of nature appears to forbid it. If no existing Terrestrial algae are able to initiate such a project, quite possibly a suitable strain can be bred in the laboratory. Or, if by then we have made progress in synthesizing life, such microorganisms could even be made to order.

I shall discuss the value of colonizing beyond the Earth later on. At present, though, I might remark philosophically that by making Venus flower, man would pay a long overdue debt. His home planet knows him as the most sinister animal that ever walked its crust, butchering, burning, poisoning, gutting, and wasting. Ought we not someday to come as the bestowers and not the destroyers of life?

Mars

Meanwhile we turn our eyes away from the Sun and wonder if Mars may not fulfill the hope that Venus disappoints.

We know that this smaller planet is no abode for us. There is general agreement that the reddish-yellow areas are desert, broken by scarps and low ranges equally bleak; and such regions cover the greater part of the surface. We know that the air is thin. The best estimates of the ground-level pressure make it about 8 per cent of Earth's. However, this wispy atmosphere contains approximately thirteen times as much carbon dioxide as ours (at the surface); the rest is probably nitrogen, a little argon, and negligible amounts of other gases—no oxygen to speak of.[13] A human who stepped out unprotected into such an environment would be unconscious in fifteen seconds and dead very soon after.[14] The meteoritic craters about which the Mariner flyby has informed us likewise suggest air too thin even to be very erosive.

Temperatures are similarly grim. Though a maximum of about 85° F. has been measured at equatorial high noon, the nights go below −100° and even, in polar midwinter, −150°. The noon-to-midnight temperatures variation on Mars is like the summer-to-winter variation on Earth.[15] This is partly due to the thinness and dryness of the atmosphere and partly because Mars gets only 43 per cent as much radiation as we do—adequate for vision and for photosynthesis, but not for real warmth. The air protects against cosmic rays; but occasionally, when the so-called blue mist (possibly a high layer of ice crystals) clears away, the Martian surface must undergo a fierce ultra-violet blast.

Recently, E. J. Hawrylewicz and his co-workers have conducted some interesting experiments in which they put microorganisms and full-sized plants under simulated Martian conditions. Their results suggest that a few Terrestrial species can live and grow there. Some other scientists question the validity of these findings, but the work goes on and a good deal has been learned.[16] Taking the most hopeful interpretation, though, one still has trouble imagining how an entire Terrestrial ecology, even a microbial one, could be transplanted.

And yet the evidence for life on Mars is so strong that probably a majority of astronomers take it for granted that the planet is not really barren.

Albeit the vapor has not been found by the spectroscope, numerous clues leave small doubt that the polar caps are water and not some other material like dry ice. They are probably thin, but they need not be mere hoarfrost as some have thought. Nor need they represent the only water on Mars. Though much was lost because of the weak gravitational field, considerable ice may well have remained—underground, as was proposed for the Moon, and perhaps even some on the surface, mingled with ancient glacial debris or covered with dust.[17] It is not altogether impossible that Mars has shallow, thickly muddied swamps.[18] Be this as it may, we know there is *some* water.

As the polar caps melt, early in the long summer (twice as long as Earth's), a wave of color is seen to move down through the dark areas and those thin bands misnamed "canals." From light gray or bluish, they turn deeper gray, black, brownish, reddish, sometimes even green. Various theories have attempted to explain this as an inorganic phenomenon or an illusion. But there is nothing to forbid the simple, natural idea that these are vegetated lands that waken to activity as the precious moisture becomes available.

Then, too, as E. Opik pointed out some time ago, it is hard to account for those patches and lines if they were not alive. Enormous dust storms are often observed to blow across the deserts. Would not any marking be buried, if they were not able to shake off or grow above the dustfall?

Of course, the dark areas may be steep highlands. Then any dust that is blown onto them may soon be blown off again. But this idea cannot well explain other observations.

Polarimeter readings indicate that the dark regions are covered by very small particles that grow in size and change color during the spring. These could well be microorganisms. The same areas show absorption bands characteristic of certain organic molecules. Finally, the markings are not static as those on the Moon are. They change shape to some degree and occasionally extend "canals." New blotches can appear suddenly in the deserts. Such behavior might be consistent with volcanic activity, but the absence of detectable water vapor probably is not. All in all, we are nearly forced to accept the idea of a certain amount of plant life on Mars.

How much, though, and what kind? Most writers depict a sparse population of organisms resembling lichens, those hardy combinations of alga and fungus, which seem able to grow under practically any Terrestrial conditions. But Frank B. Salisbury has lately shown that this idea is not really tenable.[10] For one thing, lichens exhibit no particular seasonal color changes; for another, they grow very slowly; low-lying, they would not readily emerge from a dust layer; to cover areas as large as we see, they need more water than is available, and most of them require more oxygen than Mars can supply. Finally, lichens are not primitive organisms but very complex ones—parasites or saprophytes at that. They could not live by themselves, apart from all other species, nor could they develop without simpler ancestors. But a long evolution implies more than a few kinds of plants barely hanging on to existence.

Indeed, if Mars is inhabited at all, why should there not be a fairly dense population? Adapted to local conditions, life might well flourish, perhaps not as luxuriantly as here but more than marginally. On Earth, only densely overgrown regions look dark from high altitudes; so the corresponding areas of Mars may teem with vegetation. Nor need the light areas be sterile. Our own southwestern desert looks bare from above, but down on the ground there is a rich ecology.

There are certain difficulties in this idea, notably the fact that photosynthesis consumes carbon dioxide and releases oxygen. Mars has too much of the first gas and not enough of the second for many Earth-type plants to be there. But must they be Earth-type? In point of fact, the dark areas do not have the reflection spectrum of chlorophyll. This does not necessarily rule out that substance; many Terrestrial leaves show no such spectrum either. But we have no good reason, on the basis of our present knowledge, to insist that every world's life is based on the chlorophyll reaction. Salisbury suggests that Martian plants may split oxygen out of the iron oxides that are believed to account for the planet's ground color, use it in metabolism, and return it to the iron through decay processes unknown to us. Another possibility he mentions is a chemistry based on nitrogen rather than oxygen. Less energy would be released (unless the enzyme systems are more efficient than ours), but that need not be fatal. On Earth a nitrogen metabolizer above the microscopic size would doubtless be devoured or crowded out by the stronger oxygen-users. On Mars there would be no such competition.

Other adaptations could also take place. Imagine, for example, a broad, thin leaf, black by day. This can effectively absorb sunlight. Curling up and turning pale after dark, it conserves heat energy. Even so, it freezes solid, but that need not be harmful. Some Terrestrial plants, including fairly high forms, can stand this. There could be water-hoarding mechanisms too, more elaborately developed than those we find in our own desert species.

But if Mars is not a ghost world after all—if it has a strange but vigorously growing, variegated plant life—then animals look more than probable, even large ones, man-sized or better. Are we quite sure that one line of descent among them has not developed intelligence? civilization? a high technology? Are the occasional bright spots of light we see, lasting for five minutes or so, perhaps artificial? Could the new dark area, as big as Texas, which appeared in 1954, be the result of a reclamation project?

We can ask why, if they are that advanced, the Martians have not visited us. But the question is fruitless at this point. Perhaps their space-flight capabilities lag behind ours. Perhaps they are not interested. Perhaps they did visit us briefly, a thousand years or one year ago. The possibilities are endless.

As the authors are the first to agree, essays like Salisbury's do not prove that there are intelligent Martians, or even any Martian life. But they do prove that the subject is far from closed and that the rewards of interplanetary exploration may surpass all expectation. Later we shall discuss what it would mean to make contact with another race of thinking beings. I do not really expect it to happen in my lifetime. But if it does—were any men ever as fortunate as our generation?

Beyond Mars

Meanwhile we can continue to look outward, toward the giant planets.

Between Mars and Jupiter lie the asteroids, or minor planets. (A few have orbits that take them elsewhere, but the majority are concentrated in this belt.) The largest, Ceres, has a diameter of only 450 miles; the rest are smaller, probably ranging down to mere pieces of gravel. They are scarcely the remnants of an exploded major planet. For one thing, insofar as their orbits can be traced backward, they seem to have originated from at least five parent bodies. For another, their total mass is less than one thousandth that of Earth. They are probably a stillborn world, which failed to condense because huge Jupiter, coalescing simultaneously or a bit earlier, perturbed that section of the primordial cloud too much and assimilated most of the material.

Such cold, airless rocks do not look like potential abodes of life. And yet it seems plausible that most meteorites come from this zone; and we remember the carbonaceous chondrites. There may be primitive organic matter on some of the asteroids, and we cannot be sure there is no life adapted to them. However, even a romantic optimist would not expect much more than tiny, probably microscopic organisms.

Most thinkers draw the outer boundary of the "life zone" somewhere around here. Beyond, they feel, is cold too intense for any imaginable biochemistry. Nor do the planets we find look promising in any other respect.

Jupiter, the greatest, has a diameter commonly given as 88,700 miles at the equator (83,800 from pole to pole, since its rapid rotation flattens it considerably). But this is because we are measuring the outer layers of an immensely thick atmosphere. We cannot see to the bottom, or very deep at all. Somewhere down there, we suppose, lies a solid body. According to Rupert Wildt's once favored model, this consists of a rock-and-metal core thirty-seven thousand miles in diameter covered with a mantle of ice seventeen thousand miles thick. Neither core nor mantle is in a familiar state. Under pressures less than that which must prevail on Jupiter, matter assumes strange forms. Perhaps the very crystal structure is broken down at the Jovian center, and the atoms are crowded as close together as their electron shells will allow. Whether this is so or not, the ice is squeezed into a peculiar dense allotrope. Above it there is a layer of hydrogen, forced by cold and pressure into a solid state where it behaves as a metal does.

A more recent theory, formulated by D. A. Ramsey, makes Jupiter more than 75 per cent hydrogen. (Wildt's present theories go still further in this direction.) The core of heavy elements is comparatively small, surrounded by shells of solid hydrogen whose properties vary with depth because of changing pressures. In this model, the atmosphere is less deep and weighs less heavily on the surface than it does in Wildt's earlier view. But whatever the truth is, we can be sure that the air is immensely more compressed and turbulent than Earth's. We can also be sure that it consists largely of hydrogen and helium. Jupiter is too big to have lost its primitive atmosphere. Nitrogen and neon ought to be present as well, and the spectroscope has identified methane and ammonia. The observed temperature is approximately −200° F.

Under such conditions, we must expect weird things to happen. Radio data indicate electric storms of unimaginable violence. Many workers think the beautiful colors of the cloud bands are due to free radicals—molecular fragments—which nature could never release in such quantity on Earth. That marking, thirty thousand miles long, known as the Great Red Spot, remains unexplained. One suggestion is that it may be an ice island—frozen water squeezed into an ultradense condition, tinted by strange chemicals—floating in the atmosphere itself.

Surely this is the last place we would think of looking for life. Nevertheless, John Campbell remarked once that an unprejudiced visitor to the Solar System would more likely pick Jupiter than Earth as inhabited. The former possesses a vast area, with all the diversity and the chances for lucky accidents that this implies; a huge abundance of every element; a concentration and a churning together of molecules until chemical reaction must follow chemical reaction in bewildering complexity. Earth is a mere ball of rock, its nakedness hardly covered by a swipe of water and a breath of gas, exposed to twenty-seven times the destroying ultraviolet rays that Jupiter gets!

There may, in the end, prove to be more truth than humor

in such words. The Jovian atmosphere is closely akin to that of the ancient Earth. It has retained hydrogen and helium, of course, but perhaps this does not influence chemistry too much. If there is less actinic light to energize organic molecules, there is more lightning.

But where on that frozen surface is a solvent?

A startling new retort expresses doubt that the surface is frozen. As in the case of Venus we can only observe the outer cloud layers; and for Jupiter we have no evidence, like the Cytherean radio emission, pointing directly to conditions farther down. We do, however, know that methane and ammonia vapor, such as definitely exist in the Jovian air, produce a greenhouse effect.

The ground temperature would not have to rise very much above the high-altitude value for ammonia to become a liquid, and then its solvent properties are fully comparable to those of water. But Sagan, who is the author of this suggestion, thinks it possible that the Jovian surface may even be as warm as Earth's. In that case, gigantic seas roll across the king planet, perhaps covering it altogether. In this ocean, full of dissolved carbon and nitrogen compounds, energized by lightning and, perhaps, by whatever upwelling forces create the Red Spot, life *ought* to be generated.[20]

True, the organisms would be an unearthly sort that function in a reducing rather than an oxidizing atmosphere. Perhaps they are doomed to remain forever primitive on that account. On the other hand—but that is for a later chapter. Here I will only repeat a calculation by Isaac Asimov. If the Jovian ocean is planet-wide, and has as much living matter per cubic inch as our seas do, then on this world a mass equal to one-eighth of our Moon is alive.[21]

Again we must remember how speculative this all is. But again we see how little dogmatic we dare be.

Though four of them are big, two bigger than Mercury, Jupiter's satellites are airless. So are all the other moons of the Solar System, with one exception. Therefore, as biological environments, they need not be discussed separately from the asteroids. The exception is Saturn's largest satellite, Titan, which has a thin atmosphere of methane, probably with some hydrogen and helium. The greenhouse effect cannot be strong and, the surface temperature is probably not far above that measured in the upper Saturnian air, around −250° F.

As for the ringed world, its surface conditions are presumably a colder, lower-pressure version of Jupiter's (whatever that may be!). We cannot say if life is also possible here, and we have to admit that the remaining three planets look most unpromising. If anything alive stirs in their gloom, it must be utterly alien to us.

Nonetheless, the Solar System has proven a point, which will stand even in the unlikely event that every single member of it except Earth is barren and always has been. We can no longer consider life an insignificant epiphenomenon. In fact, today that is the attitude that violates scientific caution. Looking toward the stars, we may feel sure that we are not alone among their myriads.

Chapter 4

Beyond the Sun

ALTHOUGH LIFE is no negligible accident of cosmic history, we have not yet made any numerical estimate of its importance. Nor have we decided what kinds and conditions of life are probably most frequent throughout the universe. To examine these matters, let us begin by asking what the possible environments are.

Writers on astronomy, even specialists, ordinarily divide the Sun's family into "Terrestrial" and "Jovian" planets. The former are Mercury, Venus, Earth, Mars, and probably Pluto: small dense globes with comparatively thin atmospheres or none at all, their chemical composition dominated by iron, oxygen, magnesium, and silicon. The latter group comprises Jupiter, Saturn, Uranus, and Neptune; massive but of low density, overlaid with deep atmospheres that must be largely hydrogen and helium. The two sorts are further distinguished by the fact that the Terrestrials lie close to the Sun, which makes them warmer than the frigid giants. (Pluto is an exception, but then Pluto is a freak in many respects.)

When we take a closer look, as science has lately been doing, these neat categories turn out to be misleading and, in fact, downright wrong. As for temperature, we have already seen that the Jovian surface may be warmer than the Martian; at least the question has been reopened. It is well established that the atmospheres of the big planets are not identical or even very similar. Those of Jupiter and Saturn resemble each other and so do those of Uranus and Neptune, but the two pairs are markedly different. The gaseous envelopes of Jupiter and Saturn must be far more extensive than the Uranian and Neptunian, because of their considerably lower over-all density. This in turn implies larger amounts of hydrogen and helium. Methane and ammonia have both been identified on

Jupiter and Saturn. But neither Uranus nor Neptune shows any indications of ammonia. This may be simply because they are so cold that this compound is frozen solid and thus is undetectable by the spectroscope. But temperature does not account for the fact that both atmospheres show a much greater quantity of methane than do the airs of Jupiter and Saturn. Finally, these four planets fall into pairs according to their masses. Jupiter has approximately 318 times the tonnage of Earth, and Saturn 95; but Uranus and Neptune possess a mere 14.5 and 17.2 times Earth's mass, respectively.

Turning to the inner planets, we find that the single category "Terrestrial" must also be broken down. Earth and Venus can be lumped together, but both are utterly unlike Mercury or the Moon. We are not accustomed to thinking of the Moon as a planet; but although it is not the Solar System's biggest satellite in an absolute sense, it is by far the largest in proportion to the world it goes around. Saturn, for instance, is something like three thousand times as massive as its largest moon, Titan, while Earth is only eighty-one times as heavy as Luna. The Earth-Moon system is best regarded as a double planet. Though Mercury has five times the mass of Luna, this disproportion is not much greater than that between Jupiter and Saturn. It is as reasonable to classify the first two orbs together as the second two. For that matter, Titan and the four biggest Jovian satellites are akin to Mercury.

Mars poses a harder problem. Offhand the decision whether to class it with Earth and Venus or with Mercury and Luna seems rather arbitrary. Since it has an atmosphere and, apparently, life, we are predisposed to regard it as a sister world. But if it were as close to the Sun as Mercury, it would be almost as bereft of air. From a strict geophysical—or should one say planetophysical?—standpoint, Mars belongs with Mercury and Luna because, like them, it does not seem to have a definite core as Earth does, but to be a pretty uniform rocky ball throughout.

In addition, the Solar System contains thousands of smaller bodies. And now, beyond the Sun, we find evidence of planets immensely larger than Jupiter. There does not seem to be any reason why a complete range of size should not exist, from the hugest possible star to the tiniest dust mote.

Of course, some sizes may be favored in the creation of planetary systems. We do not know of any world that fills the considerable gap between Earth and Uranus, or of any intermediate between Neptune and Saturn. But in the present state of our knowledge, we cannot rule out such possibilities. This is the more true because stars occur in all masses, down to the point where they cease being stars and start being planets.

There is no very clear-cut distinction between these two kinds of heavenly bodies. Imagine a set of objects condensing from a nebula, some big and some small. The larger ones will become stars. But as the mass we are considering becomes less, we arrive at a certain value where the interior pressure and temperature are no longer high enough to start thermonuclear reactions. However, there has been a great deal of heating due to gravitational energy release—the same kind of heating that a normal sun undergoes when it first begins to shrink—and this is enough to make the object a sphere of glowing gas. So big a sphere will not cool off for a long, long time. We can call it a star or not, just as we please.

A still smaller object will, naturally, be less heated by its own coalescence. Eventually we reach such a size that a body can form—with or without undergoing an initial molten phase—that has a cold solid center in which is concentrated a reasonably large proportion of the total material. Though it is necessarily surrounded by a vast gaseous atmosphere, we now definitely have a planet and not a star. But the chances are that this is not simply a bigger Jupiter. Although many uncertainties becloud the subject, there is reason to think that extremely big worlds like the companion of 61 Cygni are different in kind as well as in degree.

Let us therefore set up a fresh classification system. Bear in mind that it is completely arbitrary and that there are probably no gaps in the real sequence of planets. Nevertheless, we may find these categories useful, since they call attention to certain important characteristics that depend on mass. I shall follow traditional practice to the extent of centering the classes on Earth and Jupiter, but shall extend new classes in both directions.

Superjovians

Superjovian planets are the biggest, with the known cases ranging from about ten to sixteen times the mass of Jupiter. There seems to be no reason why they cannot be larger or smaller than this, the upper limit being that point at which we can no longer consider them true planets, the lower limit being when they approach the value for Jupiter itself.

All we know about worlds of this kind is inferred; we have no direct observations. But a few things can be taken for granted. The superjovians must have starlike compositions, with hydrogen overwhelmingly predominant, helium abundant, and everything else a mere trace of impurity—at least as far as percentages go.

To be sure, the heavier elements within them may amount to a very respectable absolute tonnage. And the precise composition doubtless varies, depending on the age and the galactic location of the planet, just as in the case of stars. Superjovians that are very old or that have formed in metal-poor regions, like the halo, must be almost entirely hydrogen and helium; others may have enough higher elements to affect their surface conditions noticeably. In general, though, we picture them as balls of solid hydrogen, wrapped in enormous hydrogen-helium atmospheres. By analogy with our own big planets, we may assume that they rotate quite fast and so are rather flattened at the poles.

Despite their mass, they are not necessarily as big in volume as our major planets. The tremendous gravitational force may well compress their solid cores. If the force is great enough, the very atoms are affected. Their electrons are squeezed into the lowest attainable positions, quite near the nuclei. This vastly reduces the space each atom occupies. Calculations suggest that Jupiter actually has the largest possible diameter for a planet. If mass gets any higher, the atomic crushing process begins to operate, becoming more marked with every increase in weight. A typical superjovian may be no bigger than, say,

Uranus—if this theory is correct, which some authorities dispute.

The mass certainly has another critical effect. One reason why planets like Jupiter do not have orbits close to the Sun is that if they did, its heat would boil away their hydrogen. This would diminish them so greatly that they would no longer be planets like Jupiter! But obviously a superjovian can lie closer to a star without being seriously damaged. We need not think of this class as being always bitterly frigid. (The cases we know about doubtless are, considering their orbits around dim red suns.)

Even a moderately warm superjovian seems unlikely to have life. Its atmosphere may hold a certain amount of methane, ammonia, and other prebiological compounds, but these must be so diluted by hydrogen and helium that it is hard to imagine how proper concentrations could ever build up. This judgment is not final, as we shall see in Chapter 5; but let us be conservative for the time being. Even so, I think planets like this may extend the domain of life enormously.

My reasoning is as follows: We have seen how unlikely it is that double- and triple-star systems have Earth-like attendants. Not only does it seem improbable for a small planet to form in the first place, with the nebula roiled by two or more moving stellar masses; but if it should come into existence, its orbit would usually be unstable and the planet would come to grief. However, we know that multiple systems can breed superjovians and apparently maintain them. So great a body is not unduly perturbed. Probably even a double star whose members are fairly close together—within several A.U. of each other—can have such a planet.

A superjovian's gravitational field ought to control its immediate vicinity, overruling disturbances by the more distant suns. Therefore we can reasonably expect it to have satellites. If Saturn weighs three thousand times as much as Titan, a superjovian of ten Jupiter masses should be able to stand in the same relation to its own biggest moon—which would, then, be just about as heavy as Earth. And if, in addition, the superjovian gets as much radiation from its combined suns as we get from Sol, the Earth-sized moon begins to look very homelike.

This sort of thing need not happen very often to make a big difference to the abundance of life. Probably more than half the stars are double or triple. If a certain percentage of them, even a fairly small percentage, have superjovian planets with some habitable satellites, then the galaxy has billions more fertile worlds in it than would otherwise be possible.

Jovians and Subjovians

Jovian planets are typified by Jupiter and Saturn. As I mentioned, they must lie rather far from their suns if they are to keep their identities. Of course, if the star is cooler than ours, they can lie correspondingly closer. This leads to the paradoxical thought that perhaps the smaller stars have more big planets than the larger, brighter ones.

Be that as it may, jovians* are chemically dominated by hydrogen and helium, but not to the overwhelming degree that the superjovians are. In the previous chapter I discussed briefly the chance of life on worlds like this. When we come to alien biochemistries, I must go into the matter in more detail.

Subjovians, represented by Uranus and Neptune, are even more poorly understood than jovians. But their significantly smaller mass and higher density suggests a few things about them. Evidently we cannot depict the structure of their solid globes along the lines of Wildt's or Ramsey's Jupiter models. Rather, the subjovians must have extensive stony and metallic centers, though in the case of the two such planets we know, this may well be overlaid with a thick shell of ice. The great amount of methane in their atmospheres bears out the idea that higher elements have begun to play a meaningful role in this class of worlds. That, of course, is because they are not large enough to keep hydrogen and helium in jovian quantities. (Admittedly, this observation may simply be due to our seeing deeper into their thinner atmospheres.) Presumably ammonia is also there, but frozen solid.

* To avoid confusion with the particular cases of Jupiter and Earth, the general classes "Jovian" and "Terrestrial" will hereafter not be capitalized.

If such a planet lay closer to the Sun, or had a hotter sun than ours, it would lose still more hydrogen and helium, but not all. Its atmosphere would then consist of hydrogen, methane, ammonia, and inert gases. Life as we know it could not survive there, except maybe a few anaerobic bacteria. Any oxygen released by photosynthesis would unite with hydrogen to form water, thus cutting off the plant-animal interchange at the start. (Besides, Terrestrial plants themselves need oxygen for part of their metabolic cycle, just as animals need small amounts of carbon dioxide.) But presumably life would never get to the point of chlorophyll-bearing cells anyway. The excess of hydrogen influences chemical evolution too much.

Even so, this evolution ought to follow roughly the same lines as Earth's, up to a point. Organic compounds should form, react, and accumulate. Complex structures should develop. In fact, it is hard to see why primitive cells should not appear in time, though it might take longer than was the case for Earth. Granted this, dare we say flatly that higher forms could not evolve? I shall try to prove later on that hydrogen-utilizing life is not only possible but quite probable. All in all, subjovians at reasonably high temperatures seem very likely to be inhabited.

If the temperature gets sufficiently high, all the hydrogen escapes. Reducing the mass has the same effect. In either case we get our next class of planet.

Superterrestrial and Smaller Planets

Superterrestrial worlds are entirely hypothetical, but I would be astonished to learn that they are not quite common in the galaxy. These are simply planets rather more massive than Earth and less so than Uranus, small enough to lose their hydrogen and most or all of their helium under prevailing temperatures, but big enough to keep other gases. Pluto may be a case in point if a minority opinion about its mass turns out to be correct. However, it is so far from the Sun that any "atmosphere" must be liquid or solid. We are interested in superterrestrials that get enough heat to be abodes of life.

If such a world has the same density as Earth, its radius is proportional to the cube root of its mass. For instance, if it is eight times as heavy, it has twice the diameter. The pull of gravity on its surface will then also be twice what we experience on Earth. (Actually, the chances are that the planet will be somewhat denser, because the interior minerals are forced into denser crystalline forms. If so, gravity is higher in proportion to mass.) This enables it to keep a thicker atmosphere than ours, though not a very much deeper one. This in turn ought to produce a stronger greenhouse effect. A superterrestrial getting as much sun energy as Earth might find itself in the unhappy position of Venus: too hot for life to get started. On the other hand, it could maintain comfortable temperatures at far greater distances than Earth could. This is a distinct advantage if its sun happens to be cooler than Sol.

Other things being more or less equal, we should expect superterrestrials to bring forth photosynthesizing plants, animals, and oxygen-nitrogen air. But still they differ greatly from Earth. For one thing, their life might develop even faster than it did here, because the dense atmospheres concentrate prebiological substances so much more. For another, the air they eventually have presumably contains more of everything than Earth's does. A human could not breathe it: the oxygen itself would burn his lungs, even before nitrogen narcosis and acute carbon dioxide acidosis set in.

On a comparatively small superterrestrial planet, high mountaintops might be habitable by men (if the local biochemistry is not too radically different—a problem we must discuss later). The less massive the globe is, the more congenial it should be to us, until eventually we arrive at an Earth-like situation.

Terrestrial worlds, however, are not necessarily pleasant ones. Venus proves this. We can assume that every such planet starts with an atmosphere like that of the ancient Earth. If it is fairly near the sun, and life does not develop, water vapor continues rising into the upper air, where ultraviolet radiation breaks it up. The hydrogen escapes and the oxygen attacks methane and ammonia. The upshot is a mixture of nitrogen, carbon dioxide, and water vapor, with a powerful greenhouse effect keeping the surface intolerably hot.

On the other hand, if the planet lies far from its sun, all the water is frozen solid. This does not necessarily mean perpetual barrenness. Given an atmospheric pressure, ammonia is a liquid between about −28° and −108° F., and appears to be a useful solvent. I will discuss the possibility of life under such conditions in Chapter 5. It looks like a good bet. I do suspect, though, that biopoesis in these cases is slow; and of course the ultimate result is utterly foreign to us.

A cool sun has about the same effect as a distant one. I say "about" because the temperature of a star determines not only the amount but the kind of radiation it emits. The cooler it is, the less ultraviolet light it gives off, both in absolute terms and in percentage of total output. This must influence the history of any planets. The rate at which hydrogenated molecules, like water, are broken up is correspondingly less than with a hot sun. This means fewer intermediate oxidation products, like acetic acid, generated in the primitive atmosphere. And naturally there will be less ultraviolet activation of simple organic molecules. This is no proof that life cannot arise on the planet of a red dwarf star. Besides the small amount of actinic radiation that actually is present, lightning, vulcanism, radioactivity, and flares (which will be discussed shortly) also furnish the environment with energy. But it seems reasonable to believe that prebiological evolution takes place at a slow rate, just as in the case of a bright but distant sun.

Bearing in mind, though, that life did not need too many millions of years to appear on Earth, we must be wary in using that adjective "slow." Half a billion or a billion years should be ample to produce living cells on a cool terrestrial planet. Once the event has occurred—once cells actually are there—evolution would probably speed up because by then the life is adapted to low temperatures.

A red dwarf star lasts so long that it, and any planets it may have, can easily be billions of years older than the Solar System. If life can develop at all under these conditions (and the best guess is that it can, in most cases if not in every one), then there has often been time for it to arise in such places and even to surpass us.

Subterrestrial worlds, like Mars, Mercury, and Luna, complete our list. They are considerably smaller than Earth; they lack cores, being uniformly rocky throughout, and have thin atmospheres or none. Many of them throughout the cosmos are no doubt sterile. But as we saw in Chapter 3, they cannot simply be written off. Even if Mars does not really have a flourishing ecology, there should be many Mars-like planets that do, especially if they have somewhat more mass—say, a quarter of Earth's. The example of Mars also reinforces the argument that many cold terrestrials as well as subterrestrials are inhabited.

A small planet close to a bright star must lose all its air and surface water and so, probably (if not certainly), all chance to generate life. But if the star is dimmer or the planet more distant, this need not happen. Thus the subterrestrials of red dwarf stars appear to be more important, from the biological viewpoint, than those of yellow stars like Sol. I have remarked that perhaps small suns tend to have big planets comparatively close in. But this need not rule out subterrestrials. Not only can they exist nearer to any star than a jovian, but they can be satellites of larger bodies.

If it is very cold, a subterrestrial may even retain hydrogen. Titan has apparently done so. But at those temperatures biopoesis is not a very plausible idea. Somewhat larger and warmer, a subterrestrial should exude an atmosphere similar to the ancient Earth's, though thinner. Presumably its subsequent history will resemble that of Mars. A subterrestrial still bigger and warmer might follow an Earth-like course of development.

Below this class of worlds we find the asteroids and the lesser satellites of the great planets. But I shall not concern myself with them, having already decided they are unlikely to carry anything but microscopic life, if that.

Planetary Evolution

Besides mass and temperature, a planet's over-all composition must depend on the composition of the nebula from which it condensed. We have seen that this depends, in turn, on the age and on the galactic location. The first generation of stars could not have acquired anything but superjovians; there was nothing available but hydrogen and a little helium, and nothing smaller than a superjovian can pull itself together from such light material. The same situation probably obtains to this day in the most tenuous parts of the galactic halo. But by the second generation a few planets may have been formed containing higher elements where a local supernova had enriched the interstellar medium.

This process accelerated with time. Nevertheless, the large-scale production of superterrestrial and smaller worlds appears to be a fairly recent thing. Though I have suggested that there are inhabited planets, belonging to red dwarf stars, that are billions of years older than Earth, I did not mean to say they are as old as the galaxy itself. The dense galactic center must be rather poor in worlds comparable to our own. Doubtless a good many do exist there, in absolute numbers; but the proportion is less than in the dusty spiral arms. Similarly, terrestrial and subterrestrial planets are going to be more common in the future of the galaxy than they are now—and they are evidently rather plentiful today.

One interesting possibility is that of planets whose mass is more or less Earth-like but that, being older or far out in the halo, have only very small percentages of heavy elements like iron. Their globes would be entirely of rocky material, much less dense than ours. This makes the surface gravity comparatively low. For instance, a planet with four times the mass of Earth but only half the density exerts a pull at the surface no greater than what we are used to. But because this pull decreases more slowly with altitude, the planet will retain more atmosphere than ours has done. Thus we can imagine a place of thick air and enormous horizons, whose inhabitants are still in the Stone Age because copper and iron are precious metals.

But it is not certain that any such world exists. Present theories of element formation indicate that most kinds of atoms are built up before the exploding stars scatter them into space. If so, we would not expect very much variation in terrestrials, superterrestrials, and subterrestrials. If they can form at all, they should have approximately the same compositions.

Still, even a small variation may be important to the inhabitants. A slight change in the abundance of, say, copper—which is so minor a constituent of Earth that fluctuations look statistically possible—would profoundly have influenced human history.

We can speculate about still other kinds of planets. Suppose, for example, that Luna were as big as Earth; what a night sky we would have, and what an incentive toward crossing space! I might add, prosaically, that two such bodies would generally turn the same face to each other all the time. So the companion planet would only be visible in one hemisphere, and the day would equal the month. On the other hand, there is no obvious reason why Earth could not have had several small moons rather than a single big one.

But these things are merely exotic. Let us consider more important variations. Might we, for instance, have a very hot planet with oceans of liquid sulfur? The cosmic abundance of elements makes it unlikely; oxygen atoms are about 220 times as common as sulfur atoms. The same restriction applies even more severely to hypothetical environments in which alien biologies might develop, for example, a hydrogen fluoride ocean and an atmosphere containing free fluorine. The latter gas reacts still more energetically than oxygen; but it is much more rare. We cannot say that no such worlds occur anywhere in the universe, complete with life, but we can say that if they do, they are freaks.

Later in the book I shall indulge in a bit of speculation about life under radically un-Earthly conditions. But for the present let us be conservative.

The Abundance of Life

I have discussed those kinds of planets that we can feel reasonably sure do exist and have tried to indicate how representatives of all categories except the superjovians may be inhabited—if conditions are right. But I have not yet ventured any guess as to how often conditions *are* right. To do this, we must consider the stars again, for ultimately all the energy for life comes from a sun.

As we saw in Chapter 1, it seems that only main-sequence

stars of Class F5 and below have planets.* A very large majority of these suns are cooler and redder than Sol. There are, for instance, ten times as many M stars as there are G stars. From this fact, more cautious thinkers than I infer that only a small percentage of all the planets in the universe can bear life.

The argument goes as follows: Life requires a certain range of temperatures, essentially that range in which water is a liquid. Now, a bonfire on a chilly night makes a broad circle of ground comfortable, whereas you must sit close to a little fire, though not so close that you get burned. In the same way, a hot star is surrounded by a wide region in which the temperature is right for liquid water, but a cool one has only a very narrow zone like this. The chance of a planet's orbit falling within the liquid-water zone is therefore much smaller for the red dwarf stars; and, alas, red dwarfs are much the commonest kind. In addition, multiple stars rarely allow any Earth-sized body a stable orbit. All in all, such calculations indicate that only 3 to 5 per cent of the stars in our galaxy have inhabited planets.[1]

This is still a respectable number, around five billion. We have no right to raise metaphysical objections to it, such as, So many other worlds can't simply be going to waste! There is no scientific reason to believe that life was ever intended; it is simply a property of matter under certain conditions. If one does hold, on religious or philosophical grounds, that the universe exists in order to furnish a setting for animation, it still does not follow that useful planets are an ordinary thing. Nature is prodigal enough in other respects; think of dandelion seeds or fish eggs. It would not be at all out of character for her to make a hundred worlds in order to get a single fertile one.

My argument in favor of many stars rather than a few, shin-

* Any worlds that once belonged to red giants, or to other stars now evolving off the main sequence, have either been engulfed or burned barren. Possibly the outermost planets in these systems have acquired a reasonable temperature, but the stars will not remain in their present condition long enough for this to do any good.

ing upon creatures that live and think, is strictly physical. The idea of a narrow "life zone" neglects too many factors. It neglects the greenhouse effect, which must be especially important for superterrestrial and larger worlds. It neglects the strong chance that many double stars have superjovian planets in stable orbits with habitable satellites. It neglects the likelihood, which we shall examine in more detail later, that nonterrestrial biologies exist, adapted to nonterrestrial conditions. It neglects meteoritic panspermy, a very minor process on the cosmic scale but conceivably one that adds a per cent or two by seeding globes that could not have evolved life independently.

Beyond reasonable doubt, a great many planets are dead. Whole planetary systems must be. But in far more cases, I think, even stars at the cold end of the M-range have at least one tenanted world apiece.

It follows—because small dim stars are the commonest—that the majority of living organisms exist under a redder light and a lower temperature than we do. Nor are their suns always as constant as ours. From time to time, many stars of Class M emit great flares, fiery outbursts of gas from which stream radiant energy, ions, and electrons. Sol does this too, but its normal output is so high that the flares do not make any significant difference. A similar event increases the brightness of a wan red dwarf, for a short period, as much as four or five times.

Life on their planets has doubtless adjusted to these fluctuations. Atmospheres and magnetic fields are effective barriers against the charged particles that are spat out. But the flares give us an extra reason to think that biopoesis can take place. We observed that cool stars emit comparatively little ultraviolet light and concluded that any prebiological evolution in their systems must be slow. Without changing our minds, we now see that spurts of intensified irradiation do occur. Thus given occasional boosts, matter has a greatly improved chance of increasing its complexity.

I am not prepared to offer any close estimate of how many stars have one or more life-bearing planets. But my guess, for whatever it is worth, is that at least half of them do—fifty billion or better in this one galaxy. Admittedly, most of these worlds are not Earth-like. A majority are colder and darker than our home; some are hotter, though probably not very much hotter; most have atmospheres that we could not breathe, even when they contain oxygen. But they are not barren.

As for how many stars have attendants on which a man could live without special protection, this is also a matter of guesswork. The conservative figure I cited, 3 to 5 per cent, may not be too far off. For reasons that have been given, I am personally inclined to put the figure higher, say about 10 per cent. Whichever it may be, we have, in our single galaxy, from three to ten billion worlds capable of supporting life as we know it. Every person on Earth could be given such a planet, and there might be some left over.

But we still have to decide just how similar to us the organisms on those "reasonably warm" terrestrials are; or how different. The mere fact of their being at home in an environment where water is liquid and oxygen is free does not narrow down the field very much. I ought also to justify my claim that nonterrestrial planets can be inhabited, making the total number of life-bearing worlds in the galaxy on the order of fifty billion. To do this, I must go into a little more detail about possible biochemistries.

In other words, having tentatively concluded that life is common in the universe, let us try to imagine how various it must be.

Chapter 5

Life As We Do Not Know It

IN THE IMMENSITY of space and time that has been given us, he would be foolhardy who declared that we know now, or ever can know, all the ways in which matter and energy work out their destiny. What is man, that the cosmos should limit itself to those things he can understand—at this one precise moment of his own long history, or ever?

Nonetheless, we can make predictions about the farthest galaxies and see them verified. We can postulate the existence of the near-infinitesimal neutrino, in order to save a well-established law of physics that certain radioactive atoms would otherwise be violating; and a generation later, with the technical resources that have accumulated meanwhile, we can detect the neutrino. We can be embarrassed because Piltdown man does not fit into the human evolutionary tree that we have reconstructed, and then learn independently that Piltdown man was a hoax. Altogether, we have enough experimental data and closely knit theory to think about a great many things we have not yet observed. And when scientific imagination does not go too far beyond scientific fact, its conclusions are often more or less right.

In this book I am trying to stay within that realm. Pure imagination is unbounded, but by the same token there is no way to judge the relative merits of its creations. Obviously we do not know all the manifold details of the universe: the surface of Venus or much of our own ocean beds, the animals on the second planet of Tau Ceti or in the remoter jungles of Brazil. Still, these details are governed by fundamental natural laws, like those that limit the number of ways that atoms can combine chemically.

There is no proof, and in the nature of the case there never will be any proof, that we have discovered every such law. So perhaps the galaxy is crisscrossed with the traffic lanes of a commerce that, somehow, travels faster than light. Perhaps entire galaxies are linked into superorganisms by telepathy between their inhabitants. We cannot say these things are impossible. But we can say that we have discovered no laws that make them possible. Concepts so daring belong to science fiction. See, for instance, the magnificent works of Olaf Stapledon. But this is a kind of poetry, inspired by science but operating far beyond its borders.

The speculations in this chapter, and generally throughout this book, stay closer to home. No principles of physics or chemistry are used except proven ones. That may narrow the discussion unduly. There could be many forms of life besides those I will consider. Some may be perfectly plausible ones that I have simply overlooked; others may depend on rare and special conditions, existing as a minute percentage of all the life in the universe; still others are possible if, and only if, a great deal of present-day science turns out to be incomplete or erroneous. I do not wish to be dogmatic about them. I say only that we cannot think about them today with the same precision that we can apply to more conservative ideas.

We have already decided that there are from three to ten billion more or less Earth-like worlds in the galaxy. We know from experience that such an environment can breed our kind of life: nucleic acids and proteins in water solution, with the atmosphere going through a plant-animal cycle that keeps it mainly oxygen and nitrogen. On the principle that similar causes lead to similar results, we can reasonably expect the same basic biochemistry to exist on other Earth-like planets. Of course, that biochemistry is very basic indeed. Innumerable variations of detail look possible and even probable. Later I shall examine some of them.

But let us first consider non-Terrestrial situations. So little is known about this subject that I can only offer a few general ideas in support of the claim that many such worlds must be inhabited. Most of what will be said is not original with me. The best treatment that I have seen is by Isaac Asimov, who is a biochemist among other things, and I will lean heavily on his work.[1]

It is a truism that the lifestuff anywhere must be something that can withstand local conditions. So we may imagine purely metallic creatures on the bright side of Mercury and animated ice crystals on the dark side. But these are fantasies pure and simple. Life requires extremely complex molecules, not only for the many chemical functions that even the most primitive organism carries out but also for the vast amount of information that must be stored. (This is plain enough to see in the case of heredity, where the genes furnish the information, the "blueprint," by which a new organism is built up; but the same principle applies to co-ordinating the myriad processes within a fully developed living thing.) Only carbon is known to form such configurations. As we shall see, it is barely possible that silicon has analogous properties under very peculiar circumstances, but for the time being let us stick to the one element we know will do the job. It seems quite safe to say that life everywhere—except perhaps in environments that make organic reactions impossible anyway—must depend on carbon compounds, however many chemical oddities it may employ in addition.

Life on Subjovian Planets

As we saw before, life also requires a solvent, which in our case is water; and we saw that a reasonably warm subjovian planet ought to have water in abundance, plus the simple compounds that were the raw material of life on Earth. We saw too that these materials ought to react with each other, building up forms of ever greater elaborateness and versatility. Such a process is energy-storing. Sun energy has gone to make the big molecules, and more is constantly being poured into the system; the molecules can best use the surplus by interacting to form still bigger molecules. So logic indicates that prebiological evolution will follow the same general course as on Earth until self-reproducing units arise. The question is, Must the very earliest life on a subjovian planet then use up all the organic nutrients and die for lack of ability to make more—or can it evolve something akin to photosynthesis?

In Chapter 4 I dismissed the idea of an oxygen-releasing

cycle in a hydrogen atmosphere. However, that does not mean that oxygen cannot be involved. Asimov has made a suggestion that is certainly worth investigating. If the first plants on a warm subjovian split water into hydrogen and oxygen, they could release the hydrogen and combine the oxygen with methane to form carbohydrates. (Of course, this would not be done by chlorophyll, but by some other substance.) The hydrogen excess would reduce primordial carbon dioxide to methane. Ammonia would not be affected except insofar as it supplies nitrogen for living tissues. The atmosphere that eventually resulted would contain chiefly hydrogen and ammonia —doubtless with a liberal helping of helium and traces of other gases, including some methane.

Then this balance would be maintained by the animals that eat the plants. Breathing in hydrogen, the animals would break down the carbohydrates into water vapor and methane, which they would exhale. In oxidation-reduction terms, the biochemistry of such a world is just the reverse of Earth's![2]

Naturally, it would not work without enzymes to promote the long series of chemical reactions that are involved in practice; but then, neither would our own life be possible without enzymes. The point is that from a standpoint of energetics a plant-animal cycle—plants storing energy in the form of complex molecules, animals releasing energy as they use up those molecules—makes just as much sense where there is free hydrogen but no free oxygen as it does where there is free oxygen but no hydrogen. One might almost think it makes better sense. Life arose in a reducing atmosphere on Earth too, and has had to adapt to the oxidizing conditions that later appeared. The adaptation need be much less on a subjovian planet such as we are considering.

The question may still be asked, Why should a biochemistry like this develop? But the answer is merely, Why should it not? Darwinian selection must have operated in an even more clear-cut fashion on protolife and primitive life than it has done on higher forms with their elaborate defenses against hostile environment. Any variation that was possible, and that conferred an advantage, rapidly perpetuated itself.

It may be that, for one reason or another, the variation Asimov proposes is not a possible one. But it is by no means the only system we can imagine. An equally plausible notion is that plants use sunlight to build up not carbohydrates but higher unsaturated hydrocarbons. In digesting these vegetable products, hydrogen-breathing animals saturate them and break them down again to the original simple compounds, notably methane. The advantage of this concept is that it seems reasonable for planets so cold that water is permanently frozen but ammonia is liquid. This class is an extensive one, including many frigid bodies of subterrestrial and higher mass, on up through jovians.

Life on Cold Planets with Hydrogen Atmospheres

The physical and chemical properties of liquid ammonia are closely akin to those of liquid water. Specific heat, heat of evaporation and fusion, solvent power, and ability to liberate hydrogen ions—all extremely important to biochemistry—are nearly as high in the former substance as they are in the latter. Ammonia does have one drawback. Its solid state is denser than the liquid. "Ice" forming in lakes or seas will sink to the bottom and therefore be slow to melt when the weather warms up again. Many planets such as we are now discussing no doubt have permanently frozen ocean beds. But this is not fatal. There should be enough overlying liquid to support life all the time. Indeed, the congealed bottoms will help stabilize planetary temperature, which may be no small advantage if a planet's sun is a red dwarf prone to flaring.

Ammonia oceans need not be terribly cold in any event. Perhaps there are numerous planets where this liquid seldom freezes at all. For at a greater than Terrestrial air pressure, such as is found on the larger worlds, the boiling point of ammonia rises above −28° F. We have already discussed the case of Jupiter, and how much warmer it may be under the clouds than above them. Given conditions like that—liquid ammonia, a hydrogen atmosphere with organic impurities, and an energy-supplying sun—we once again expect pre-biological compounds to accumulate and elaborate until life appears. And why, then, should these earliest cells not "learn" to use a sun-powered saturation-unsaturation cycle, thus developing plant and animal kingdoms?

Three objections can be made. First, hydrogen-carbon reactions yield less energy than do oxygen-carbon reactions, weight for weight. Second, although subjovian atmospheres must be reasonably transparent, the air of jovians is so dense that not enough sunlight penetrates to allow photosynthesis or any equivalent. Third, a subjovian must be very cold (or its hydrogen would escape, making it a superterrestrial) and, therefore, complex organic reactions cannot take place anywhere near fast enough for the subtlety and variety that life requires.

These are all perfectly valid arguments, but they can be answered. As for the first point, it does not show that life is impossible in a hydrogen atmosphere, only that it will be more sluggish than oxygen-utilizing life if other things are equal. An animal might creep along by our standards but live at a perfectly normal rate by its own. However, other things never are equal. Anyone who has watched a slow loris in a zoo and then gone next door to a cageful of monkeys—its rather close relatives—will appreciate how much difference a slight physicochemical change can make. There is no known reason why enzymes should not develop to promote the reactions of hydrogen with carbon compounds until they are equivalent to the reactions of oxygen. This is the more true when we reflect that just because hydrogen does react less energetically than oxygen, it hangs on to a molecule less doggedly; so there might well be more reactions going on per second within our hypothetical organism than go on within ourselves. Finally, the air is so dense near the surface of a big planet that each lungful of it contains a great many more hydrogen atoms than a lungful of Terrestrial air has oxygen atoms. This again compensates for the lower energy yield.

The second point is admittedly a disturbing one. Though a world like Jupiter must have plenty of infrared radiation if the surface is warm, probably little visible light, or none, straggles through the atmosphere. Conditions must be analogous to our deep-sea beds, where life is sparse and depends on whatever drifts down from above. Carrying on the analogy, one might suggest that there is an ecology in the higher levels of air, at altitudes where ultraviolet light does penetrate though the cold is not too intense. But if any such layer exists at all, the chances are that it can only support microscopic life.

Yet we cannot press this idea too far. Life on Earth is ill adapted to the ocean depths; and we have seen that alternative biologies cannot arise because their precursor molecules would be destroyed by oxygen and microbes. This is not the situation on a young jovian planet. Energy sources like lightning do exist there, presumably clear down to the surface; and perhaps these activate a prebiological evolution. It would take place much more slowly than on Earth, especially if the surface is cold after all—but it may still happen. And in that event, Darwinian selection will favor those molecules that are less stable than the biological molecules of Earth. At our temperatures, under our degree of irradiation, such compounds break down very quickly. Under the conditions of a jovian planet they would last; yet they would be just unstable enough to enter into complex reactions. Infrared light might even serve for photosynthesis; or, if not that, we can fall back on lightning, far more common and energetic in so vast an atmosphere than it is on Earth.

However, I cannot make any specific suggestions about these molecules that are supposed to take the place of our nucleic acids, proteins, carbohydrates, and the rest. Therefore, I do not insist that jovian planets *must* be inhabited. I feel that many of them are, but at present I only wish to show that this idea cannot be dismissed without a far more detailed scientific investigation than has yet been made.

The third point concerns subjovian planets cold enough to retain most of the hydrogen they would otherwise lose. But this argument that organic reactions are too slow at such temperatures for life was answered in connection with the first and second points. Appropriate enzymes, and molecules with just the right degree of stability not only might arise but probably would. A planet on which ammonia is a liquid, but which is well below Jupiter in gravitational power, cannot have a terribly dense atmosphere. So light penetrates, sparking organic evolution and eventually photosynthesis. Nor need we talk as vaguely about the carbon compounds as I did in the case of a jovian. They should be closely related to our own. After all, Terrestrial life survives temperatures around −100° F., given comparatively minor adaptations.

Life at Extreme Temperatures

As the planet gets colder still, ammonia eventually freezes solid. But methane is a liquid (at Earth's air pressure) between −259° and −297° F. This is a narrow range, and it is not easy to imagine evolution succeeding on a world where the oceans boil or freeze with slight shifts in the weather. The range can be considerably extended, though, by a greater atmospheric pressure. Then too, the temperature of an ocean-sized liquid mass does not change as readily as the temperature of air.

If methane is present in the liquid phase, it will not dissolve the same kinds of materials that water and ammonia do. Biochemistry could not be based on proteins and nucleic acids. But methane will dissolve lipids—a class of compounds including oils and fats—and lipids can form molecules, right here on Earth, whose complexity is comparable to that of protein. We do not know if a self-reproducing lipid structure could arise, especially in the cold and gloom of a liquid-methane environment; but at the present stage of our knowledge we cannot say it is impossible. Hal Clement has even proposed, fictionally but in considerable detail, that life of this sort may exist on superjovians.[3]

Asimov suggests that liquid hydrogen may also dissolve lipids. On such a basis, we can imagine strange inhabitants of a world like Pluto, not far above absolute zero. But the energy shortage, not to mention the fact that most other substances will also be liquid or solid, makes the idea frankly rather far-fetched.

Turning to the other end of the thermometer, is life at very high temperatures chemically reasonable? Ordinary organic compounds break down when they get less hot than they would on Mercury's bright side. However, fluorocarbons—analogues of the hydrocarbons, with fluorine atoms replacing hydrogen—are extremely stable because the chemical bond is so strong. At some temperature they may become just unstable enough to furnish a possible starting point for prebiological evolution. The problem is what to do for a solvent. Asimov proposes liquid sulfur. Perhaps a minor sea or some good-sized lakes of it exist, if not on Mercury or Venus, then somewhere in the universe. By virtue of being small compared to Earth's oceans—thanks to the low cosmic abundance of sulfur—these bodies might concentrate fluoro-organic compounds all the faster. Of course, we do not know that chemical evolution would then build up larger and larger molecules, but the idea seems worth a careful study.

One objection to it is that fluorine is a rare element in the universe. But this need not be fatal. Here on Earth, phosphorus is absolutely essential to life, which carries out energy transfers within the cell by means of the organic phosphate ATP. Yet this element is also among the minor constituents of matter.

Carbon is not quite the only sort of atom that can form giant molecules. Boron is not dissimilar, but it is another rare element. Silicon, which is abundant on the smaller planets, looks a bit more promising—not by itself, but in combination with oxygen. These two elements, symbolized by Si and O, respectively, hook up to form long molecular chains: —Si—O—Si—O—Si—O—. When a methyl radical (a carbon atom attached to three hydrogen atoms) links itself to either side of each silicon atom, we get a chain like this:

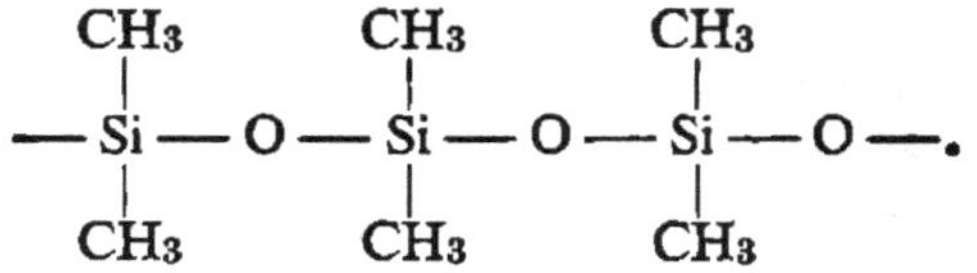

$$
\begin{array}{ccccccccccc}
 & CH_3 & & & CH_3 & & & CH_3 & & & \\
 & | & & & | & & & | & & & \\
— & Si & — & O & — Si & — & O & — Si & — & O & —. \\
 & | & & & | & & & | & & & \\
 & CH_3 & & & CH_3 & & & CH_3 & & &
\end{array}
$$

This general class of compounds is known as the silicones. They are distinguished by both stability and versatility. Perhaps there are hot environments where silicone-based life occurs.

Alternatively, Asimov suggests that fluorine may substitute for hydrogen to form the hypothetical "fluorosilicones." Simple molecules of this kind, remaining liquid at elevated temperatures, might act as the solvent in which more elaborate ones can evolve.

But all this has gone further afield than my purpose entitles me to do. Such ideas are fascinating. We have glanced at the possibility of lipid life in liquid methane or liquid hydrogen, fluorocarbon life in liquid sulfur, and silicone or fluorosilicone life on planets where the rocks glow red-hot. Other published speculations include the living nebulae Hoyle described in a novel;[4] organisms that get their energy from radioactivity or even from nuclear fission; chlorine or fluorine breathers; and much else. But all this lies beyond the scope of the present book. The main reason for bringing it forth is to show how little we can afford to declare what the limits of life really are. At present, science cannot say much more about these concepts than has been said here.

Life Somewhat As We Know It

On the other hand, a great deal can still be said about protein-based life. *Mutatis mutandis,* many conclusions drawn about this kind can be applied to the more hypothetical sorts. Let us therefore return to the class of environments in which the development of proteins is very probable.

We can go so far as to say that on Earth-like planets proteins are inevitable. By "Earth-like" I mean all worlds too small to retain hydrogen or helium but large enough to retain other gases, and with temperatures in that range where water is usually a liquid. They include terrestrials, subterrestrials larger than Mars, and superterrestrials, provided that the temperature meets our specifications. Because superterrestrials can remain warm even when receiving appreciably less solar energy than we do, they must be especially important in red dwarf systems.

In addition, I feel confident that certain other kinds of planets are inhabited. Warm subjovians ought to have liquid water and a protein-based life that uses hydrogen, perhaps in Asimov's carbohydrate cycle. Cold subjovians ought to have liquid ammonia and a protein-based life that employs hydrogen in something like the hydrocarbon cycle that was discussed earlier.

This leaves us with the interesting intermediate case of planets cold enough to have liquid ammonia oceans but small enough to lose their hydrogen even at those temperatures. Not all the water will be frozen solid; much of it will be contained in the oceans as part of the ammonium hydroxide molecule. Under such conditions life might develop an analogue of photosynthesis as we know it, with ammonia substituting for water; or it might even develop an oxygen-carbon dioxide cycle similar to ours. (Though carbon dioxide is itself liquid through the lower half of the liquid ammonia range, there should be some vapor in the air.)

In an oxygen-carbon dioxide cycle, the free oxygen would attack the ammonia, and the oceans would slowly be converted to gaseous nitrogen and frozen water. However, this process must be slow indeed—the more so because solid ammonia sinks and is thus protected from the air. Life should have ample time to adjust to the change, at least up to a point. Nor need it go to suicidal completion. One obvious biological adaptation to a dwindling ammonia supply is the development of a nitrogen-fixing metabolism that produces more of this compound. In that case, a stable situation will eventually be reached. The planet's air will be composed of nitrogen, oxygen, some ammonia and carbon dioxide vapor, and trace materials. The surface will be extensively covered with frozen water, but a certain amount of liquid ammonia will remain.

In summary, then, it looks like a rather safe bet that most planets with masses ranging from, say, twenty-five times to one-half times Earth's, and with average temperatures ranging between about +150° and −100° F., develop protein-based life. On the larger worlds this life operates in an atmosphere containing free hydrogen, on the smaller ones in an atmosphere containing free oxygen. On the warmer worlds the liquid medium is water, on the colder ones ammonia.

This greatly extends the range of life more or less comparable to ours. Subterrestrials huddling close to red dwarf stars; superterrestrials and subjovians feebly irradiated but maintaining a powerful greenhouse effect; superjovians protecting giant satellites from orbital instability in multiple star systems —possibilities like these supplement the conventional "right size planet at the right distance from the right kind of sun," and that conventional category itself turns out to be quite broad.

There, then, is my justification for holding that at least half the stars in the galaxy must have at least one attendant each on which there is protein-based life.

But we cannot get much more specific than this, except in the case of the *strictly* Earth-like worlds, that is, globes approximately as big as our own that receive approximately as much sunlight. So now I shall narrow the inquiry down to this class.

No doubt its organisms use many familiar types of compounds, not only proteins and nucleic acids but also carbohydrates, lipids, and others. Biopoesis seems to allow for nothing else. Yet we must not be too dogmatic. We have already seen that sheer chance probably determines many crucial details, such as whether *d*- or *l*-amino acids predominate. Likewise, it seems plausible that genetic material on such a world is always a nucleic acid; but I know no reason why it has to be just the DNA we use. Quite probably, intracellular energy transfer generally involves a phosphorus compound, but not necessarily ATP. Biochemists can speculate along such lines for hours if they wish.

As for physiology, one might ask if large organisms must always be composed of distinct cells. The answer seems to be, Yes. The square-cube law would too severely handicap a single giant cell in its quest for nourishment. The closest we have on Earth to any such thing are the slime molds, confined to damp environments where organic matter is already present. Like the viruses, they seem to be comparative latecomers in evolution, dependent on higher forms to provide their nourishment. There are so many advantages to being multicellular that once such life forms have arisen, even the most primitive, they soon take over the realm of anything above the microscopic.

But might not very small and complex organisms exist? If so, they probably have correspondingly small cells. This in turn means that each cell, below a certain size, is more simply organized than one of our own. There are fewer molecules to go around. That militates against the idea of an advanced creature. Besides, although small cells can still perform the functions of life—down to a point—they grow increasingly more vulnerable to random effects, such as chance chemical encounters and spontaneous molecular readjustments.

The tiniest cells known on Earth are the pleuropneumonia-like organisms. They have only a hundredth the diameter of a typical mammalian tissue cell. The theoretical lower limit, beyond which thermal effects are too great for the structure to survive, is about half this; and such a life unit would exist on the brink of disaster. A man composed of pleuropneumonia-like cells would be less than an inch tall. But he could not be a man as we understand humanness. For one thing, the huge surface-to-volume ratio would produce more heat loss through his skin than his metabolism could cope with. Furthermore, there would not be enough genetic material to carry all the specifications of so elaborate an organism.

As a matter of fact, there is remarkably little variation in the cell sizes found in the tissues of macroscopic Earthly life. Cells from corresponding organs of different species rarely vary by a factor of more than two or three, and even cells from different organs fall within this order of magnitude. This suggests that it is the best size range.

We cannot state flatly that a smaller type—say a tenth as big—could not have developed instead, and has not developed elsewhere. But the idea is pretty speculative. Though pure chance accounts for much at the molecular level of organization, can it operate to any such extent in the evolution of something as large and complicated as a cell?

Of course, on a colder planet there are fewer thermal effects to disrupt the structure, and in fact a bit more instability might be advantageous. So perhaps the frigid worlds tend to develop life with smaller cells and correspondingly smaller multicellular organisms. But again, the need for chemical complexity must set a lower limit, especially for higher forms of life. An intelligent being from a liquid-ammonia planet might weigh only ten pounds, but it is hard to see how he could weigh as little as half a pound. At the other end of the scale, the square-cube law and the force of gravity put an upper limit on cell size, which is probably not much higher than the limit we observe on Earth.

The chemical products of cellular activity must be various indeed throughout the universe. Men landing on another Earth-like planet would have to be very careful, for many common substances—after billions of years of separate evolution—would doubtless be violently poisonous to them. Even here at home, quite apart from defensive materials like snake venom, we have hay fever, botulism, laurel hells, and such unpleasantness. Also, no doubt many otherwise harmless biological products on the foreign planet would stink to high heaven according to human noses. (But one can get used to mere odors.) By the same token, men need have little fear of extra-terrestrial microbes. It would be easier to catch alfalfa wilt than most alien diseases. In the rare cases where an exotic germ did attack humans, it could only produce a limited number of effects, since the body is only capable of reacting in a limited number of ways. (Thus, the numerous kinds of influenza have much the same symptoms.) A future science capable of transporting us to the planets of other stars will surely be able to deal with any syndrome.

But despite these multiple differences of detail, I think we can specify the possible kinds of metabolism on Earth-like worlds, at least in broad outline. By "metabolism" I mean the set of chemical processes by which living organisms obtain energy and convert the materials available to them into the materials that they require. It is clear that life cannot keep going on a planet unless some types develop that synthesize complex compounds and store up energy surpluses. Sunlight being the only important energy source, these types must be photosynthetic, that is, plants. But then mutation and natural selection are bound to produce other forms that utilize the first kind, and thus we get animals.

To be sure, we do not know if oxygen-releasing photosynthesis always involves chlorophyll or even a very closely related compound. But we can predict, according to the laws of chance, that on many planets it does. Likewise, although the energy consumers in an Earth-like environment carry out oxidation reactions, the word "oxidation" in its technical sense does not necessarily imply any use of free oxygen. The best-known example of this is fermentation, in which organic compounds such as sugars are converted to other organic compounds such as alcohols and acids, and carbon dioxide is released. There are bacteria that get their energy from inorganic substances, for example, by converting sulfur to sulfuric acid. The nitrogen-fixing bacteria are a case of tremendous importance to the entire planetary ecology.

But all these metabolisms are far less energetic than the familiar system that uses free oxygen to "burn" organic compounds into carbon dioxide and water. Thus, when this process operates on grape sugar, it releases over twenty-four times as much energy per gram as does the fermentation of grape sugar to ethyl alcohol. The advantages are obvious, and it is no accident that every animal of more than microbial size is an oxygen utilizer. Conceivably, on planets like Mars alternative metabolisms have developed comparable efficiency. But on Earth-like worlds they probably never get the chance to do so. The oxygen utilizers crowd them out too early in the game.

As for the chemistry that handles this violently corrosive gas, here on Earth we have more than one kind of molecule that carries it to the tissues where it is needed—notably hemocyanin, the blue copper-based substance that crustaceans use. But hemoglobin like our own is the most efficient carrier we know, and the iron it contains will be readily available on all terrestrial planets. So I think the majority of animals throughout the Earth-like fraction of the universe employ compounds that are at least roughly similar to hemoglobin. But since their blood may carry highly colored materials, it need not always be red.

Considering the truly fantastic variety of size, shape, and function that we find on our own world, one dares not predict what possibilities life may be realizing elsewhere. However, it is worth noting that the real biological oddities—by human standards—are found among the lower, and especially the smaller, species. A zoologist or bacteriologist would be in paradise if he could take a microscope to another planet. But the big, highly developed creatures of most interest to the ordinary man will probably run to pattern.

For instance, a grazing or browsing animal needs jaws suited to leafy matter, which means it cannot have teeth like a carnivore's. If it relies on fleetness for defense, as antelope do, it must have a slender build, and usually a rather long neck to help it watch for enemies. If, on the other hand, it elects to fight off predators, it must be big and equipped with formidable weapons—horns, tusks, perhaps a spiked tail like the old stegosaur's—but not the carnivore's fangs and claws, since these would interfere with its normal routine. The bigger the animal gets, the stockier it must also be to carry its own weight. Compare sheep, cattle, and pachyderms.

Naturally, these engineering considerations leave wide scope, as the zoology and botany of Earth bear witness. Chapter 6 will go into a little more detail in connection with intelligent beings. To sum up what has been said thus far: life on the more or less Earth-like worlds must itself be more or less Earth-like. Its chemistry is based on nucleic acids and proteins, its physiology on cells. There are plant and animal kingdoms whose species will eventually fill every ecological niche. Let us next inquire how often evolution produces creatures that think.

Chapter 6

The Appearance of Intelligence

"WE SHALL HAVE TO GANG WARILY," said Simon Templar on a memorable occasion; "but nevertheless we shall certainly have to gang."[1]

Thus far in our attempt to sketch the biological side of the cosmos, we have had powerful tools. Though much is unknown and much else controversial, the principles of astrophysics, chemistry, and biology are at once precise and widely applicable. We can use them with some confidence to determine what broad ideas are probably correct and what false. But when we come to the finer details, these principles are no longer of use, and those we must employ instead are much less potent. Paleontology is not an exact science, anthropology is an almost entirely empirical one, and psychology cannot yet be called a science at all. Exciting discoveries are being made in these fields, but they still lack the breadth and unity of concept that identify a mature discipline. Most likely they always will. Any predictions made on the basis of what we know, or think we know, about these subjects are correspondingly uncertain. Yet it is the only basis we have on which to reason about intelligent life on other worlds.

We cannot say flatly that such life *must* exist. There is no scientific evidence that nature strives toward the goal of consciousness, or indeed toward any goal. On the contrary, the fossil record speaks strongly against such beliefs. Anthropomorphically viewed, evolution consists largely of false starts, grotesque blunders, and endless repetitions of the same mistakes. To mention only one example, species after species has fallen into the trap of overspecialization and become extinct when conditions changed. The exquisite adaptations of living organisms result from brutal winnowing of the less fit. Most of nature's failures are dead and gone and therefore escape the average person's notice, but they vastly outnumber the successes. Man himself is not exactly a master stroke. Any doctor can tell you at length about the design flaws in us, both mechanical and nervous.

But these remarks are cynical only if we insist on making them in human-centered language. Let us rather think of life as one manifestation of an infinitely various, marvelous, and beautiful reality. This attitude need not conflict with religion. Most churches have long ceased to make pronouncements about material nature. Barring a few crank cults, I do not know of any faiths that lay down dogmas about other planets.

Though we lack a priori proof that consciousness is not a rare accident of evolution, we would naturally like to think so. To us, one man is worth many sparrows, and one planet that houses beings who wonder about the stars is worth hundreds populated only by dumb animals. But wishes are no substitute for logical investigation.

The Gestation Period of Intelligence

At first glance, geological statistics might appear to dash our hopes. Protoman—an animal using primitive tools—may have existed two million or so years ago, but this is a very small fraction of Earth's age. And Homo sapiens is scarcely more than a hundred thousand years old, probably younger. If we assume that there are fifty billion life-bearing planets in the galaxy, but that intelligence occurs throughout space in the same proportion as it occurs in Terrestrial time, then there are approximately a million races comparable to man in our own stellar system. The pessimistic guess mentioned earlier, that only some 3 per cent of the stars have even one inhabited planet, shrinks the number of worlds with sentient beings to about sixty thousand. Of course, when either of these figures is multiplied by the total of galaxies in the universe, the result is impressive. But the percentage remains dismayingly low.

However, such reasoning is most confused. Intelligence does not appear at random, with any million-year slice of time being as likely for the event as any other. It is the result of a long process. We do not know how long. Obviously the time required is considerable, but must it be as great as on Earth?

If a climatic upheaval had wiped out the dinosaurs a hundred million years ago, might not the great efflorescence of mammalian life have taken place correspondingly early? On the other hand, it is conceivable that evolution on Earth has been abnormally fast. Worlds with a less turbulent geological history might have a less rapid turnover of dominant life forms.

I have suggested that on the planets of red dwarf stars, biopoesis may be comparatively slow; and they appear to be the commonest sort. Yet we have also seen that a great many of them must be far older than the Solar System. This should counterbalance and eventually overbalance any effects of a low-energy environment.

As for Earth-like planets, the one on which we happen to live took the better part of its sun's lifetime to produce reasoning animals. Sol is unlikely to stay on the main sequence as long in the future as it has done in the past. So perhaps many worlds, otherwise more or less like ours, "fail" to evolve sentience before they perish. This may be true especially often of planets whose stars are brighter than Sol and therefore shorter lived. Though greater irradiation might hasten the appearance of living cells, this will, in general, not compensate for the much shorter time span in which the world is habitable.

These considerations are not as glum as they sound. Accident probably steps up the pace of evolution as often as it causes delays. Several million years either way means little geologically but a great deal biologically—and everything historically. There must be many more factors determining the course of life's development than just the mass of a star.

We have every reason to think that however the time scale may vary from place to place, evolution will follow certain general patterns: those that confer ever greater advantages in particular environments. New phyla, orders, families, genera, and species will appear, flourish, die out, and be succeeded by improved organisms. One tendency that we can trace through paleontology is for certain types of life to develop increasingly better sense organs and more elaborate nervous systems.

This does not mean that they form the main line of evolution. It has no main line. As a matter of fact, microbes and insects not only outnumber the vertebrates but outweigh them. I am only pointing out that in the immense ecological variety, through time as well as space, that must exist on any inhabited planet, there are pretty sure to occur niches that an animal with a good brain can fill. Such animals—quick-moving, quick-witted, sharp of eye and ear, not overly specialized but able to live under many different conditions—have been abundant on Earth since the Tertiary period began, if not before. It is hard to see why life everywhere in the universe should not in time reach some equivalent of this stage. To pin it down further, let us identify it in our case with the Miocene, about twenty-five million years ago, when the mammals were in their glory and our simian ancestors had become a noticeable feature of the African landscape.

In trying to guess how much time another planet might need to get this far, we will probably not be wildly wrong if we assume that Earth is about average. When we deal with astronomical quantities, the different accidental factors cancel each other out. If our assumption is right, then half the life-bearing worlds have reached their version of the Miocene epoch or gone beyond it. According to my earlier estimate, this means that some twenty-five billion planets in our single galaxy have animals with complex nervous systems. Admittedly this is guesswork. Reduce the figure to a half, a third, or a tenth, if you please. The number is still enormous beyond imagining.

The Birth of Intelligence

So it looks as if the biological potential for sentience is common enough. But we have yet to show that this potential will normally be realized. The evolution of man is not at all well understood. There are theories aplenty about it, but none that really satisfy us. The advantages of having an ability to learn by experience, rather than being bound to the inherited behavior patterns of instinct, are obvious. Many animals have developed some intelligence. But why did the process go so much further in one family, the hominids?

The idea that the ice ages forced our ancestors to learn the use of tools and fire was naive from the first, and has been thoroughly exploded by the discovery that protoman had both in regions that always enjoyed warm weather. A more modern school of thought holds that primate sexuality, operating the whole year round, was a precondition for the development of a large brain. The fact that the male was constantly in the presence of the female, and thus gave her his protection, made possible a long period of helpless infancy—which an animal requires if it is going to depend more on learning than on instinct.[2] Another theory is that during the twelve-million-year drought in Pliocene Africa, one variety of ape left the shriveling forests for the savannah and took up hunting, doubtless after a carrion-eating stage. Here it was advantageous to travel on the hind legs only, which let the forepaws become true hands. Poorly armed by nature, the ape learned to use thighbones and sharp jawbones as weapons—our first tools.[3]

The subject is exceedingly obscure. And we are not certain why intelligence evolved as far as it did. Java man already had fire and chipped stone, and was a successful animal on that account. What pressure was on him to develop further? One is almost forced to conclude that intraspecies competition became fierce. It could not ordinarily have taken the form of war. Primitive hunters must work too hard for their living to organize really vicious attacks on their neighbors. But the more clever kinds of hominid, with more efficient social organizations, could multiply until they crowded out the slower-witted types. Within the tribe (if we may give that name to pre-Homo sapiens groups) there may also have been selection in favor of intelligence. Perhaps it was largely sexual. If chattering, roaring, and other noisy behavior attracted the female —as plumage or dancing does in the case of various birds— then those males that were the most inventively talkative would beget more than their share of young. This quality is associated with the ability to think abstractly, as well as with the positive human need to communicate on which Susanne Langer has remarked at length.[4]

But such ideas belong in other books. I mention a few of them here only to show how little we can be certain of about our own origin. How much less can we say about the genesis of nonhuman races light-years distant from us! I doubt that the same causes, whatever they were on Earth, operate throughout the cosmos to produce rational beings. Given a "Miocene" state of things, there is probably an immense variety of circumstances that can favor the development of intelligence.

Granted, this development requires a series of accidents: climatic changes, or geographical displacement of a species, or whatever else might work to put a premium on brains. But decisive accidents are very likely to occur, though chance decides just which ones do. Consider how the pace of Earthly evolution has increased with time. It took something like two hundred million years to go from the trilobite-dominated Cambrian ocean to the first fishes; sixty million years from fish to the first air-breathing animals; perhaps twenty-four million years from the ape Proconsul to the erect tool-using Australopithecus (if these species are not in the same line of descent, their close relatives must be); and a million or so from Australopithecus (or his similar contemporaries) to us.

The skeptic may retort that this acceleration is illusory. The evolutionary steps are not equivalent. The transition from fish to amphibian involves enormous changes, whereas the difference between one bipedal primate and another is biologically trivial. That is true, but it is the exact point I wish to make. By the Miocene epoch, nearly all the work of evolution had been done. Enormous stretches of time were not necessary for the rest of the job. Perhaps if whatever accidents were involved had not occurred, there might still be nothing higher than apes on this planet. But in the course of a few more million years, would other crucial events not be likely to occur?

On such grounds I feel reasonably sure that most inhabited planets, if not all, will eventually bring forth creatures that reason. Twenty-five billion worlds in this galaxy, as I have suggested, may at some time have reached the point where intelligence is the next important step in evolution. I think the great majority of them have already taken that step. In short, this galaxy may very well contain some twenty billion races equal or superior in thinking ability to us. Again, you can be conservative if you wish and reduce the number by a high percentage. It still remains large. Not only is life common in the universe, but intelligence is.

Animal Versus Vegetable

What will extra-Terrestrial intelligent life look like? Will it be so fantastically alien that we could not even recognize it as such, or will it be strictly human? The most reasonable answer lies between these extremes.

Obviously the natives of worlds that are quite unlike Earth must be quite unlike man. Apart from his inability to breathe hydrogen, drink liquid ammonia, or survive the cold, a six-foot two-legged human is mechanically poor on a typical subjovian. Heavy gravities would seem to favor beings that are short and broad, often with more than one pair of legs. In contrast, a very tall, thin, mantislike leaper might have distinct advantages on a subterrestrial. But we cannot go into detail. The ramifications are too many.

However, it is feasible to reason at some length about planets fairly similar to Earth, and a few of the conclusions may be applied to other environments. This was done by L. Sprague de Camp, with wit and verve as well as scholarship, more than twenty years ago, when only the science fiction magazines were giving any space to such problems.[5] Much of what follows in this chapter is based on his long article, as is the latter part of Chapter 5.

Brain does not develop for no reason at all, but because in some manner it gives its possessors a survival advantage in the particular conditions under which they live. This rules out intelligent plant life. Fixed in place, a tree or bush would gain nothing, either of protection or of food-finding ability, if it could think. One might ask, What about plants that are able to move around? But a study by V. A. Eulach disposes of that idea. A photosynthesizing man could only produce a few per cent of his energy requirements. The more he was modified so as to be a better energy producer or a less greedy consumer, the more he would approach a purely vegetable condition.[6] With a caveat to be discussed later, we can take it for granted that all thinking beings are animals, and motile animals at that.

Size and Habitat

Intelligence does not appear in any shape at all, either. It is limited to forms that are capable of being its carriers. This is a tautology, but imaginative writers often overlook the principle. For instance, the animal cannot be too small, or it will have too few cells for the many nervous interconnections that thought requires. We have dealt with the matter of cell size already. Although we reached no final conclusion, it did seem probable that cells on Earth-like planets must be approximately as big as those on Earth. They might vary by a factor of two or three, of course, perhaps even more; but whoever wants to make them very much larger or smaller has a great deal of explaining to do.

The minimum number of cells for an intelligent animal is uncertain. Human midgets demonstrate that the total can go considerably below our norm without affecting the mind. De Camp's guess at the lower limit for Earth-like environments is forty or fifty pounds. Bearing in mind the different things that can vary, a smaller being is theoretically possible. But if the creature gets too diminutive in relation to other animals, intelligence is again of no great value. Humans six inches tall would be gobbled up by predators in spite of their weapons. They would do better to specialize in speed and hiding ability. Man himself is actually a giant animal, the vast majority of species being smaller. Altogether, fifty pounds looks like a fairly good guess at the minimum.

As for the upper limit, the protointelligent creature cannot get too big, or it will be unable to move about briskly and encounter the variety of challenges that make brains valuable. We do not know if a tree-dwelling stage is essential, as some have suggested. Our own arboreal ancestors are very remote; apparently we are descended from ground apes. But it may well be that the initial impetus toward developing a really good nervous system comes from some such difficult environment as the treetops. If so, this probably eliminates thinkers the size of elephants, whose line of descent was surface-bound for countless ages. On the other hand, the breed might start small and evolve into something bigger, as the horse has done on

Earth. De Camp thinks a ton or so is about the maximum weight.

True, a sea-dwelling animal can get indefinitely large and remain nimble. The whales bear witness to that. But the sea is too monotonous an environment for a complex brain to serve much purpose. In fact, as marine biology knows, evolution is extremely slow in the ocean, and ancient forms survive interminably. Granted, the dolphins are highly intelligent, perhaps second only to man. But they are descended from land dwellers. As we shall see when we come to the question of hands, one cannot readily visualize any use for an increase in dolphin cleverness—which may well be doomed to slow deterioration.

Structure and Metabolism

A fair-sized, active land animal needs support for its body. Many invertebrates have solved the problem by growing an exoskeleton, a hard exterior shell. But this is a clumsy system. It makes the animal relatively inflexible, it must be shed at intervals to let the owner grow—during which time he is nearly helpless—and it tends to insulate him from the multitude of sense impressions that a brain is meant to deal with. Internal skeletons are much superior, not only to shells but to several other methods of stiffening, both actual and imaginable. Of course, the bones need not be chemically identical with ours. (On some subterrestrial planets, perhaps muscle alone is sufficient, and octopuslike beings can walk around freely. Perhaps.)

The giant insects of horror movies are quite impossible. For one thing, the cross-sectional area of their legs is inadequate to support their mass: the square-cube law again. Furthermore, they would suffocate. An insect does not breathe, in our sense, but allows oxygen to circulate through tubes in its body called tracheae. Some, like the wasp, do pump air in and out by rhythmic abdominal contractions. But the tracheal area of a man-sized insect, or even a bird-sized one, would be totally inadequate to aerate the volume of its body. A true lung is not a mere sac, but has a complex structure that gives an enormous surface. Evidently our extra-Terrestrials must possess something similar.

(A passive tracheal-type system might work under the tremendous air pressure of a large planet, especially since hydrogen diffuses very rapidly. And maybe there are beings on subterrestrial worlds that get along without breathing at all. Compare the ideas about Martian life that were discussed earlier.)

Unless the planet has had a steady mild climate for geological ages, a homeothermic (warm-blooded) animal has every advantage of liveliness and adaptability. Even without climatic changes, such creatures are best suited to extremes of both heat and cold. Able to survive variety in the first place, they get the most good from any improvement of the nervous system. We cannot be sure that there are no poikilothermic (cold-blooded) philosophers in the Earth-like parts of the universe, but if so, they are probably rather rare.

Reproduction and Diet

The early date at which sexual reproduction was "invented" would alone prove to us that it confers tremendous benefits; but they are plain to see. The genetic reshuffling serves racial progress so well that bisexuals have taken over most of the animal world above the microscopic level. Even among bacteria we find a primitive form of sexuality, known as transduction. Thus intelligent life everywhere doubtless has sex. Here on Earth, the distinction between male and female grows progressively sharper as we move up the evolutionary scale. This is unlikely to be an accident, so I think it is generally true of other planets. The normal thinking animal will not be hermaphroditic, nor change sex routinely as the oyster does. We can imagine occasions when more than two sexes developed. The consequent increased variability of the young might offset the added difficulty of finding mates. But if this is possible, there must be an upper limit, and not a very high one, or the procedure will get too cumbersome. We manage very well on Earth as we are, and nature seldom creates superfluous organs. Therefore, I think that bisexuality is overwhelmingly dominant in the universe, and that any hypothetical exceptions cannot have more than three or four sexes. (Paramecia do, but they are microscopic.)

Since the essence of intelligence is that behavior is more learned than innate, a long period of parental care is indicated. Metamorphosis like a butterfly's, completely rebuilding the organism, would presumably destroy the memories of childhood; even the less radical amphibian version separates the generations by an environmental barrier. Thus the young of intelligent beings, though helpless at first, must grow steadily rather than make violent changes of body type and must be under adult tutelage. Egg-laying is not incompatible with this. But live birth is less wasteful of fetuses, hampers the parents less, and allows more time for the development of a complicated nervous system. This is because the fetal food supply is not limited to what can be packed within an egg. So I believe most rational animals are placental or have structures that perform a similar function. However, I do not see why milk should always be necessary. The parents might regurgitate food for the infant, as birds do; or the infant might tap the adult bloodstream through a specialized organ; or still other systems might be evolved.

It seems reasonable that extra-Terrestrials will, as a rule, be omnivorous as man is. Leafy matter contains so few calories that herbivores must spend most of their time simply eating. Carnivores are more apt to specialize in fighting ability than in intelligence. But no doubt there are many cases that do not fit this rather vague principle, especially since there is no sharp distinction on Earth between "herbivores" and "carnivores."

Shape

As for the extra-Terrestrials' means of getting about, we can imagine methods like somersaults, air jets, or wheels; but they are such bad biological engineering that Terrestrial nature has never come up with them for its larger animals. The various ways to swim are not relevant to land dwellers, which on Earth have developed three different kinds of locomotion: walking, flying, and crawling. The last of these, being too slow, is not suitable for a really active creature. Even the fastest snakes can only travel at about four miles an hour. Under very special conditions, intelligent crawlers might develop; but they would be freakish.

If the atmosphere is no denser than Earth's, a winged thinker is implausible. To get off the ground, the organism must be too small to carry a good brain. But on larger planets, where the air is thicker—even in proportion to gravity—the evolution of "cherubim" seems possible. This would likeliest be by way of ancestors analogous to our flying squirrels; birds lose the ability to manipulate, which is of no value to them. The flying extra-Terrestrial would scarcely look like an angel. A small, slender body with a jutting keelbone, batlike wings, hind feet specialized for grasping branches, forepaws become hands, a tail, and a nonhuman face—all suggest more the traditional devil, in appearance if not in personality. Yet it is a practical shape, which the herald on a Christmas card is not.

The alert reader will have noted that such a being has not four limbs but six. We almost have to postulate this, or what would the creature do for hands? An evolving brain is of scant use unless it has some means of translating its decisions into action. Australopithecus, his brain case hardly bigger than an ape's, was already making tools. This in itself must have been a powerful stimulant to the evolution of higher intelligence. The more gifted artificers had a greater survival advantage. All in all, we can feel sure that every extra-Terrestrial has some equivalent of hands.

Maybe on certain planets there are animals with boneless tentacles ending in fingerlike appendages. Our elephants have a crude version. But in general, it seems easier to modify an existing pair of limbs. Evolution as a whole usually takes the easiest course, just because those species that do so, develop faster and thus crowd out the competition. No vertebrate on Earth has more than four true limbs. So apparently on most worlds where the higher animals are quadrupeds, the intelligent beings are bipeds as we are. (They may hop rather than stride provided such constant jarring is not too hard on a large brain.)

I know no reason why the ancestors of vertebrates should not have evolved six limbs, except that it was not necessary.

On larger planets with a strong gravitational pull it might well be. Happenstance might produce hexapods on Earth-like worlds too. In that event, the liberation of the forelimbs—their transformation into arms—leads to a centaurlike being. The liberation of the middle limbs might be involved in the development of flyers, the front ones becoming wings. A four-armed biped may also be possible, but seems awkward to me. Hands on the rear limbs seem utterly impractical.

The minimum useful number of fingers is three per hand, set at right angles to each other. The maximum is probably about seven or eight. More than that would get in each other's way. For similar reasons, I doubt if eight-limbed vertebrates occur on terrestrial planets. (But some large worlds may have natives who faintly resemble caterpillars.)

It is desirable to have the principal sense organs in the forward part of the body. Even when fleeing, an animal has more need to know where it is bound than where it has been. Furthermore, these organs are best located near the brain to shorten the time needed for reaction. Within the realm of established scientific fact one has trouble imagining senses that we do not already have, at least for environments like our own. Thus we can expect our extra-Terrestrials to possess heads with eyes, ears, mouth, and nose. In some cases, the organ of smell may be placed in knobs or stalks, as it is for moths. Then the nose would presumably be lacking.

Keen eyes are a certainty because light carries so much more information per second than any other stimulus. These will not be faceted, like the compound eyes of insects. That is actually a crude system, incapable of showing fine details. Rather, the eyes will resemble ours; and the properties of electromagnetic radiation and atmospheric transmission are such that these organs will use approximately the same frequencies. But the range of vision need not be identical with man's. The wave length to which the eye is most sensitive will depend on what color is most in evidence. For us it is yellow-green, the hue of sunlight filtered by leaves. I would expect beings that live under red dwarf suns to see a distance into the infrared frequencies and not to see blue at all. The eyes might be on short stalks, though this seems more vulnerable than our own scheme. Two eyes are necessary and sufficient for stereoscopic vision. We cannot say that no beings have three or four. But somewhere around that point the law of diminishing returns would surely begin to operate.

Likewise, two ears are necessary for binaural hearing. The advantages of having more than two are slight or nonexistent. They need not sit on the head just where ours do. I believe that they will generally have external flaps of some kind—it makes for better hearing—but would be astonished if these looked like a man's. Similarly, nose and mouth can be quite strange in appearance—up to a point. The placement of all these organs need not be in the same relationship as those of humankind.

In fact, there are innumerable characteristics we cannot specify. Some would be very striking to the observer (color, tail, hair or plumage, comb or wattles, etc.) but trivial to the biologist. Others would be highly important.

We can list our conclusions somewhat as follows: The intelligent inhabitants of Earth-like planets, and many others, are land-dwelling, lung-breathing animals with internal skeletons, somewhere between a terrier and an elephant in size. They have heads, sense organs, and hands comparable to ours, however different in detail. If four-limbed, they are bipeds, and this is the commonest type on terrestrial worlds; but six-limbed centaurlike and cherublike beings are not impossible as far as we know. Usually they possess some form of internal temperature regulation, have two sexes, and bear their young alive—though they need not be placental mammals in any strict sense.

The less like Earth the planet is, the less these concepts apply and the more alien we can expect the natives to be. But their anatomy will always make good biological sense in their particular environments.

Free Imagination

So far, most of these speculations are de Camp's, with some additions and modifications of my own. The reasoning is so cogent that I feel sure its results are true for a vast number of actual cases. But must they be universally true? Can we not imagine plausible evolutions, even on similar worlds, whose outcomes are radically different?

It has been done occasionally, by science fiction authors who regard articles like de Camp's and Eulach's as challenges. Harry C. Stubbs has recently made a survey of such literature.[7] One story actually did bridge the gap between animal and vegetable.[8] Stubbs summarizes the idea: "The chief character was a being about six inches tall who grew up attached to a tree. After separating from this parent he spent a good deal of his time resting in the sunlight with widespread extensible membranes which contained a black pigment which was a much better sunlight absorber than our chlorophyll (detailed chemistry unspecified). The two square feet of membrane provided enough photosynthetic activity to keep his tiny body in fuel. He soaked up water through his skin whenever he could get it. . . . The factor responsible for selection for intelligence in his species was presumed to be the changing environment resulting from soil exhaustion by the parent trees, which were the asexual generation of an alternating system like the hydra's. The resulting difficulty of the motile, sexual generation in finding a suitable spot to plant its seeds provided a problem which might well select for any intelligence which happened to be there."

Of course, so minute a being could not be rational if its cells were comparable to ours. But they might after all be much smaller and simpler. Conceivably the mind depends more on the interconnections between nerve cells than on their interior complexity. If so, an organism made up of viruslike particles can perhaps develop reasoning ability. A Hal Clement novel makes such a species symbiotic with another type of animal; in effect, the former supplies the brain for the latter.[9]

I myself once proposed a more cautious version. A large animal, vaguely like a gorilla, was in partnership with a small, somewhat crablike being that tapped its bloodstream and could link the two nervous systems together at will. The relationship had begun as parasitism but evolved into a true symbiosis, with the big animal furnishing strength and hands, the small one brain and keen eyes.[10]

There are enough such ideas, more or less carefully worked out, to give us pause. We cannot deny that they have actual counterparts wildly foreign to humanity. But as far as we can see today, their development requires rather special conditions that are not likely to be common on planets akin to Earth.

In fact, many intelligent races must look very much like humans, "at least to somebody who does not see very well and cannot find his glasses," as Willy Ley once phrased it. There may even be a few—a very few—who resemble us almost exactly. But such a coincidental relationship can only be skin deep. Anatomists would find innumerable differences. Still more fundamental is the divergence of biochemistries after billions of years of separate evolution. No matter how large the universe, we are stretching the probabilities if we suppose that people exist on any other world with whom we Earthlings could beget children.

Chapter 7

Other Minds

FASCINATING THOUGH IT IS to inquire about the biological possibilities of extra-Terrestrial intelligent organisms, the answers are not crucial. If ever we made contact with such a race, we would be less interested in how they looked, what they breathed or ate, than in their psychology. How might they think, feel, and behave? How well or ill might we get along with them?

Some people who have speculated about this matter have decided that nonhuman thought may be so alien as to be incomprehensible to us. What strange motivations could a Martian have? What abstractions from his experience, so absolutely unlike our own, must a Jovian make, and by what rules of logic does he use those symbols? Even on an Earth-like planet the minds might be so foreign that communication is impossible.

Laws of Discourse

Though we are still more vague about psychological than evolutionary laws, I believe a certain amount of deduction is possible even in this tricky field. Thus we can forget about totally nonhuman logic (using "logic" in the strict sense of the formal principles that govern symbol manipulation). Two plus two always makes four, no matter what kind of brain is doing the arithmetic. A properly constructed syllogism always leads to the same conclusion.

This claim is not as bold as it looks. Work in the nineteenth and twentieth centuries proved, first, that mathematics is a branch of logic. Any mathematical theorem can be put in arithmetical terms, and the principles of arithmetic are largely deducible from logic. Then it was further proved that the laws of logic itself can all be derived from four postulates.

These are childishly simple. The first of them is merely "*p* or *p* implies *p*," where *p* is any statement. ("If it is raining or it is raining, then it is raining.") Actually, they are definitions. Taken together, they define what we mean by such terms as "and," "or," and "implies."

If any reader thinks he can set up different postulates and so derive a different logic, he is welcome to try. But I will give long odds that he will fail to construct anything workable, that is, any system that can be used to make deductions. For example, if he denies the first principle that was just mentioned, this will be tantamount to saying that *p* can be true and/or false. In other words, he will be denying the principle of noncontradiction. But a system incorporating that denial can equally well "demonstrate" any proposition to be true or false. Therefore it is a system that cannot really prove anything.

Of course, the extra-Terrestrial is not obliged to use logical rules. Most people do not, except in a fuzzy and semiconscious way. Logic deals with abstract, artificially simplified propositions. The statements we make in real life are much more complicated. Is monarchy a good or bad form of government? Well, now, that all depends.

But to the extent that discourse can be broken down into a set of simple true-or-false sentences, logic can handle them and handle them powerfully. Science and mathematics are proof of this.

Accordingly, we should be able to communicate to some extent with any nonhuman race. They might not agree about the facts, but they could be made to agree on the consequences of any assumed facts. This is hardly different from the situation on Earth today. A Christian, a Hindu, and an atheist may dispute strongly what is the essential nature of the universe. But if they are all reasonable men, they can follow each other's trains of thought and reach agreement on just what the areas of disagreement are.

Moreover, they could all be scientists, in complete accord about their work. Though ideology does influence thinking even in this department, one's religion or politics has nothing to do with whether or not an experiment produces a given result. The same is true of most everyday affairs and should apply to communication between men and nonhumans. Environments differ tremendously, but all environments reflect the same fundamental laws of nature.

I am not saying that a dialogue between species would be easy. It might be exceedingly difficult. But I cannot see why discussion of logical and scientific matters should ever be inherently impossible. And the adjective "scientific" covers a wide range, down to the most mundane questions. An anthropologist does not share the habits, preferences, and beliefs of the tribes he studies. But this does not prevent him from comprehending what he sees. With an imaginative effort, he can reconstruct the primitive people's mode of thought; he can, however imperfectly, make himself look at the world through their eyes. To a lesser degree, I think, this kind of empathy can be achieved with most nonhumans.

All in all, the notion of "incomprehensibly alien" thought is more impressive than meaningful. Undoubtedly some very strange patterns of instinctive behavior will be found among the lower animals on other planets. We have them aplenty on Earth. But intelligence is, by definition, liberated from instinct. Its protean character indicates that communication between species will always be feasible if both are willing to make the effort. We may not like what we learn; we may fail to enjoy their music, understand their poetry, or approve of their ideals; but we can talk about matters of practical and scientific concern.

Emotions

Bearing in mind that intelligence does not come out of nowhere but evolves from lower types of nervous activity, we can go a step further. I think that other races will, in general, have the same positive need that we do to create symbolic structures and communicate them to others. We do not engage in even the emptiest chitchat for no reason at all; it is a ritual, and rituals are a form of communication. Any person with a moderately good brain has an urge to go beyond this and actually discuss something. Creativity, whether it be of the mind or the hands, likewise demands expression. In a delightful little essay, Clarence Day once suggested that our desire to chatter is nothing but an expression of our ancestral monkey nature.[1] But I feel that this is a reversal of the truth. Simians run through a gamut of sounds and gestures, not because they are simians, but because they are among the more intelligent animals. Dogs, cats, seals, dolphins, elephants, crows, and several other bright species show similar behavior. They do not necessarily use the voice, but a dog who lays his head in your lap as you sit at dinner and looks pathetic is most certainly performing an act of communication.

If the earliest pre-men had lacked an "impractical" tendency toward playful fooling about with noises and things, I do not see how they could have invented the first crude tools. Many animals will use a stick or stone for some given purpose, but man is the only one that modifies its shape with the help of another inanimate object. How else did this practice originate, if not as a more or less idle changing of material forms, an alternative to the more or less idle changing of sound forms in throat and mouth? The chipping of a flint is just as much a symbolic performance as the uttering of a word. We have already seen that once this symbol-making tendency became well established in protoman, it probably created conditions that favored its own further development.

I have trouble imagining any way different in principle by which intelligence could evolve on other planets. Of course, the circumstances and the results need not be identical with ours. A given race might not use its vocal apparatus as much as we do. Conceivably it never uses sounds at all but depends on some other code. But I do think that if they are sophisticated enough to understand the notions involved, other races will practically always have many individuals among them who are not only able but eager to communicate with us. On the same evolutionary grounds, I feel pretty sure that these beings are—more or less—as curious, artistic, playful, and dreamy as ourselves. (The overt expression of these traits, and their intensity, might well vary from planet to planet.)

Although the foregoing chain of thought looks convincing to me, I am the first to admit that it is not a solid proof. There may after all be intelligent species with whom we could never find common ground. Improbable though it seems, one can visualize antlike races, where individual personality does not exist and the concept of extraplanetary life is literally not thinkable. Or one can depict a race stupid in human terms yet immensely gifted in some field other than reasoning power: music, for instance, though the conditions that would give survival value to such an ability are hard to imagine. Weirder psychological patterns than this have been postulated in science fiction, and I am not so dogmatic as to throw them out of court. Perhaps they exist, or things exist that we cannot even conceive.

By the same token, though, we cannot today talk very meaningfully about them. Besides, we know that the basic human pattern works: here we are! Surely there are a great many other worlds on which it has also developed. We need a special name for such beings: those with which we have enough in common mentally that intensive communication is possible. This has nothing to do with their appearance or metabolism, nor with the kind of civilization they chance to have at the moment. The reference is only to a certain cast of mind: logically reasoning, imaginative, communicative, with individuals who show creativity, curiosity, and playfulness. To escape the implications of words such as "manlike"—implications that somehow these beings do resemble us physically—let us coin a new word: "androde" (from the Greek *ανδρωδης*, "like a man"). The class of androdes may or may not be identical with the class of all intelligent beings. I suspect that, at the very least, androdes are in the large majority.

Behavior Patterns

The concept is still a very broad one. It tells us nothing about matters like sexual and religious life, inherent pugnacity or peacefulness, sociability or solitariness, indeed any of those details that would most strike a visitor. But man is so variable, and understands himself so little, that we lack an adequate factual basis on which to reason.

I do think that the sexes throughout the universe tend to specialize psychologically as well as physiologically. Among humans the male is usually more aggressive, more given to thinking in abstractions, more prone to alter and innovate, than the practical down-to-earth female. It makes good evolutionary sense. The male is expendable; the female, who must bear the young and do most of their early rearing, is not. Feminists may cite all the exceptions they please, because I am only speaking in generalities. Yet such generalities condition our history as a species. If this psychological division of labor was of racial use to man, it should be to most androdes.

Offhand, I am also inclined to think that most such beings act toward their brethren much as we do. It is certainly advantageous to belong to a species that cares for its wounded and sick. Even Pithecanthropus did this, as is shown by serious bone injuries that healed. The owners must have gotten help while they were disabled. A degree of altruism is therefore built in, so to speak. It must be so for all androdes, or their race would perish before it had time to become fully intelligent. Yet the Pithecanthropoids were also cannibals now and then, and long before them, Australopithecus slew his own kind. We have the remnants to prove it. Freed from the strongest bonds of instinct, but descended from animals that had a hard struggle to survive, androdes at our own stage of evolution may usually be aggressive, greedy, cruel, and shortsighted —even as you and I. Diverse cultures on each planet may clash, with robbery, war, and exploitation.

But although this tension between mercy and ruthlessness no doubt exists on many worlds as it does on Earth, we cannot be sure that it is universal. We simply do not know enough about our own past or our own nature. When I wrote of us as not being shackled by instinct, I meant only that our overt behavior—our responses to particular situations—are not predetermined by heredity. We are not born with a knowledge of Latin or a wish to become physicists. But reason alone never supplies motivation. It is, in truth, only the handmaiden of animal urges. In this psychoanalytic sense of "instincts," we most certainly have them, and intelligent species all do.

The trouble is, in spite of a great many sonorous theories, we do not really know what our instincts are. The Freudians make sexuality a prime force driving the human psyche. But is it? Apes in a zoo show a preoccupation with sex, which Freud also observed in his *fin de siècle* Vienna bourgeoisie.

But apes in the wild have so much else to do that sexual activity occupies little of their time. What evidence we have suggests that the analogy holds for man. Without wishing to minimize its great historical importance, I often wonder if Freudian psychology, insofar as it exists at all, may not simply be an occupational disease of Western civilization.

Are we actually descended from carnivorous primates, who have bequeathed us a positive drive to kill; is our basic desire to seize and defend a piece of territory; is the evolutionary purpose of our intelligence simply to perfect our weapons? Robert Ardrey has ably popularized the case for believing exactly this. Yet the case is by no means proven. We do not have the typical biochemistry of full-fledged carnivores. History, archeology, and anthropology alike record enough instances of prolonged peace to support an equally convincing argument that war and its concomitants are more the result of invention than instinct. We do not know. And therefore we cannot tell what buried urges might drive the dwellers on other planets.

We can guess. A herbivorous race might be more socially minded and less prone to kill its own members than we are. A carnivorous race might instinctively live in rather small groups, so great empires would not occur in its history. Some species may be less preoccupied by gadgets than we are. Others may innovate far more rapidly than we do, without the bad psychological consequences of social upheaval that man must suffer. In the present state of our knowledge, we cannot deny such possibilities as these.

To complicate matters even more, we humans differ enormously, both as individuals and in our cultural patterns. The same species produced the gentle Eskimo and the wild Apache. The same nation brought forth Goethe and Hitler. When Day fantasized about cat-men and elephant-men, he described beings that were, respectively, not very different from Cesare Borgia and some stolid Dutch burgher. There is no reason to doubt that the vast majority of androdes, probably all of them, exhibit a corresponding variability. So we cannot even try to deduce the general course of history on other planets.

Too many unknown factors, too many elements of sheer chance, are involved.

Elder Races

We can, though, speculate in a few limited fields. A particularly interesting and significant problem is that of races older than ours. Though we can say nothing about the details that would interest a historian, we can make a few guesses as to the general trend of their development. Over periods of a million years or more, it would seem that everything that can happen to a species on its home planet must happen.

So the first question to ask is whether any older races do exist. Sol is brighter than the average planet-bearing star, which presumably helped biopoesis on Earth get an early start; and yet Sol was well into middle age before man appeared, being today roughly half as old as the galaxy. But the first generation or two of stars could scarcely have had anything but superjovian planets, with so little carbon available that life never arose even if it can do so nowadays on this kind of world. So apparently Terrestrial life has been around somewhat longer than the average for this galaxy.

But there are other galaxies older than ours. And there must be planets within this one that formed before Earth, with less than superjovian mass. The time difference need not be very great, astronomically speaking. Were all planets just the same age, a few million years either way in the advent of intelligence would make no difference geologically but every difference to their inhabitants.

So we can feel sure that the universe does contain androdes who have existed longer than Homo sapiens, although they are in the minority. Maybe some of them are savages yet, that is, dependent for their food on what they can find in nature. (This would not forbid their having a very high nonmaterial culture if nature is so generous that they can take plenty of leisure time.) Perhaps metals are scarce on the older planets.*

* Whether or not the inner cores of worlds with less than jovian mass are ever metal-poor, the surfaces of subjovians may very well be so.

In that case, the tendency of the inhabitants to linger in a "stone age" must be quite pronounced.

However, many other races must have gone on to new modes of life. Sooner or later, maybe taking a million years of recorded history to do it, they have developed science. Even in a state of metal shortage, this could be done, using such dodges as ceramics, plastics, and electrolytic solutions for conductors. It would be slower and more difficult than it has been on Earth—a process we will examine in Chapter 8—but given sufficient time, a physical knowledge that exceeds our own could be achieved.

Now, the chances are that these older androdes are concentrated toward the galactic nucleus. The average age of stars there is greater than in the arms (though extremely ancient suns do occur throughout the galaxy) and so is the number of stars in a given volume of space. Dense globular clusters, whose members are separated by light-months rather than light-years, are quite probably common in the central region.

Be this as it may, the galactic heartland must contain numerous planetary systems that belong to older suns than ours, and that are relatively close to each other. Once space flight has been mastered on any such world, interstellar travel is not as hard as for us, out here on the thinly populated fringe. Later I shall try to prove that flight between the stars is possible even from Earth. If you will take my word for that for the time being, you will no doubt agree that in the central region different races will surely come in contact, and have in fact already done so. The stimulation this has given to their scientific and philosophical development must be enormous.

I cannot offer any estimate. But it does seem that there are a number of species, in this galaxy as well as others, whose knowledge and power far surpass ours. It is a humbling but wholesome thought.

Cultural Evolution

Have they also surpassed us morally?

In trying to answer that question, we tread on very thin ice. But again, a few guesses can be made. Certain people believe that every race eventually ages and becomes extinct. But there is no evidence for this idea. Exceedingly ancient life forms are still flourishing on Earth, for example, the fern, the shark, and the cockroach. Extinct varieties were usually wiped out by changing conditions or by natural enemies—circumstances that intelligence is well designed to cope with.

Some gloomy souls have wondered if every race must commit suicide shortly after it discovers atomic energy. But this also I doubt very much. For one thing, I do not expect man to do so. He will probably batter himself rather badly, but his chances of survival look reasonably good. For another thing, there is no proof that all androdes are warlike. Even if they are, they need not come upon atomic energy at such an unpropitious time as we did. If the world in 1945 had not been polarized between two great hostile social systems, there would have been no insuperable barrier to arranging international control of the atom. Or the invention might have occurred in an era when one nation dominated the planet and used the atom to strengthen that imperium. Several other possibilities come to mind. Thus man is simply unfortunate in the timing of this particular thing. There must be many worlds where it all worked out more luckily.

Still other thinkers hold that every species is doomed to the kind of turbulent but spiritually stagnant, overpopulated and undernourished existence that Sir Charles Galton Darwin foresees for us.[2] But he ignores too many possibilities that are always open. The mere fact that he says radical social changes cannot be made to stick does not prove it. His thesis rests in large part on the argument that population control methods will breed out of the race those types that that do not especially want children, replacing them with those that have a powerful urge to reproduce. But this assumes that philoprogenitiveness is genetically determined, which most geneticists do not believe—at least not without many reservations. As P. B. Medawar has pointed out, so many human traits depend on a combination of different genetic elements (heterozygosity) that social selection can only influence them to a limited extent. At present, he emphasizes, we simply do not know enough about long-range trends to make any sure predictions about our biological future.[3] Furthermore, the thousands of years required to produce even a minor biological alteration are a tremendous time-span historically. If social conditions have not changed of their own accord, changing the selection pressures as they do, human reason will have ample time to perceive the situation and take whatever steps are appropriate.

I do not wish to denigrate Sir Charles's interesting work. Books like his are a healthy antidote to fatuous optimism. I merely want to state that whatever the fate of some unlucky planets, there must be others that have maintained reasonably progressive civilizations for extremely long periods of time.

This is not to confuse progress in general with progress in science and technology. The abolition of judicial torture and of chattel slavery were forward steps as great as the discovery of Newton's laws or the invention of the electric motor; in one sense, they were far greater strides than these more material innovations. The fact that much of the world has slid backward, reviving old horrors in the name of the almighty state, does not make less real the progress that was once made and can be made again.

Yet because we are so uncertain about nonhuman psychologies, we can say little about the events that constitute moral and cultural advances on other planets. There might, for instance, unlike the case on Earth, be a subvariety of androde so retarded mentally that enslavement by a more highly developed type would prove beneficial. Progress in knowledge and technical capability is, by and large, not as equivocal. Furthermore, it seems less easily reversible than social progress.

Nevertheless, if older races exist and have learned much that is still unknown to us, I think this knowledge must include some methods of biological and social engineering. Even humankind has learned a few useful lessons from history—learned, for example, that pure democracy of the Athenian type does not work and that a dispossessed proletariat is a threat to the body politic. We have evolved, if not consciously developed, a few crude techniques for coping with some of our problems. Give us a few more centuries or millenniums, and we should have a far better comprehension of our own nature and more control over events. I would not like to live in a fully planned society, in the doubtful event that such a thing is possible. But this does not mean that unnecessary evils can never be abolished in a reasonable way.

Presumably the older races—a number of them, anyhow—have done this. They may very well be free of war, poverty, tyranny, ignorance, gross injustice, disease, perhaps even mortality. But have they on this account become basically more intelligent than we? Are they as far beyond us mentally as they are culturally?

Evolution Beyond the Androde

I am inclined to doubt it, again on the grounds that intelligence is not a mystical goal of nature but an evolutionary development serving pragmatic ends. Once a safe, orderly environment has been fashioned, what *biological* value has a greater intellect?

Let us consider it in terms of our own future.[4] Clearly we are under little or no pressure to evolve further physically. We do have many built-in flaws, such as the vermiform appendix, but they do not threaten the race—or the individual much, in this day of drugs and surgery. Evolution may clear up some unfinished business by itself, even under civilized conditions. (If the people with really bad appendixes are saved, who would otherwise die before they could reproduce, this vestigial organ will accumulate unfavorable mutations and atrophy all the faster.) Man may consciously make some other improvements, less through the impractical and dictatorial schemes of eugenics than through direct genetic control. This prospect should somewhat allay the fears of those who believe that medicine is saving the weak and thereby causing the entire species to degenerate. On the whole, though, there is no point in making radical bodily changes. Our machines can always outdo us in every physical respect, no matter how hyperathletic we become.

But what about our mental capacity? Man's brain has enabled him to become the supreme animal on Earth—outside the microscopic realm. But only the hardest struggle between individuals, prolonged for many generations, would give any noticeable advantage to the genius over the average man. (It would also put a premium on innate ruthlessness, so that the eventual "superman" would be even more vicious than his twentieth-century ancestor.) Such highly personal struggles are a rare and short-lived phenomenon. It is normally organizations, clans, tribes, countries, empires, and societies that clash. Even the so-called free-enterprise system has involved companies rather than single persons.

When anarchy does occur, the strong, intelligent men quickly gather followers and build up disciplined groups. The superior gang—superior more in effective organization and sound leadership than in gifted members—wins out. Historical cases in point include the medieval Icelandic republic and our own hillbillies. And after a relatively short time a still larger organization (the Norwegian crown, the state government) stepped in and knocked the feudists' heads together.

But will not competition between groups select for brains, if only in the leading classes? I'm afraid not. We are developing artificial supplements to our intelligence as well as to our muscles and senses. The oldest of these is probably writing; the abacus and the slide rule are quite venerable; now we have electronic computers, tomorrow we will have Lord knows what. A battery of specialized tools can do most jobs better than slowly evolving flesh. Victory will go to the side with the best robots. Insofar as human qualities are important in war or less violent conflict, they tend to be courage and steadiness of purpose rather than intellectual complexity.

What about intrasocietal competition? The qualities emphasized by it vary from culture to culture, but as a rule, within any organization, ability at politicking and at sliding between gaps in the regulations makes you more rich and powerful than does any ability to think abstractly.

In fact, throughout past history, victorious collectivities have soon begun to discourage creativity. The people on top are satisfied with the status quo and do their best to freeze it. Their underlings slide meekly into a groove that offers, at the minimum, status security. If the collectivity happens to be a great empire, it often takes outside invasion to destroy the ultimate petrified culture, which otherwise (as in Egypt and China) persists virtually changeless for thousands of years.

Roderick Seidenberg goes so far as to suggest that the world society of the future will, in the course of millenniums, destroy first individuality and then consciousness.[5] I myself do not expect matters will ever go that far. Man is not that kind of animal. His Caesarisms hold the germ of their own destruction. But it cannot be denied that there has been a strong anti-intellectual tendency in all human civilizations to date. There is some reason to think that the average IQ has declined in the past few generations and is still going down.[6] Though this process cannot continue indefinitely, it may result in a noticeable lowering of the intellectual norm. This does not mean there will be no more geniuses, only that they will be fewer in proportion to the morons.

Of course, conditions changing through the centuries can force the average up again. A long period of world-wide unrest and hardship would presumably do so. Less drastically, society might take measures to encourage the propagation of the intelligent and discourage the propagation of the stupid. I am not being alarmist about the situation, only trying to show that once a certain level of intelligence has been achieved, there is probably no further natural selection to increase this quality. In fact, our own brains are no different from those of Cro-Magnon man, and the difference between us and the Neanderthal type has been much exaggerated.

One might speculate about artificial selection, either through breeding for intellect or direct genetic manipulation of some kind. Perhaps this can be done, but not easily. We have bred plenty of species for this or that characteristic, often with great exactitude. The typical result has been a freak, unable to survive without elaborate human care: a cabbage, a pouter pigeon, a Holstein cow. Some of the less thoroughly bred animals can go wild successfully, but then they take only a few generations to shed their human-imposed traits and revert to the efficient form of dingo, alley cat, mustang, razorback. I wonder if we would have any better luck breeding for high intellect. We would probably get an inferior sort of computer, devoid of vigor and emotional warmth, domesticated and victimized by the wild-type men whose genetic balance had not been tampered with. Or if we bred a man too gentle to fight, he could well prove too effete to explore, create, and reform.

Although it is admittedly dangerous to reason about other races on the basis of humankind alone, I think these arguments are fairly general. They boil down simply to this: that there is no selection pressure to increase intelligence above a level comparable to ours; that once the androde goes from savagery to civilization, any natural selection there may be tends to work against intelligence; that by virtue of possessing artificial aids to the mind, the civilized being has no practical motive for raising his race's power to think abstractly; and that if he does try to do so, for essentially esthetic reasons, he risks upsetting the subtle balances established by millions of years of evolution.

On the other hand, technological civilization is putting us under severe emotional stress. To some extent this is unnecessary and can be alleviated. Frenchmen have fewer nervous breakdowns than Americans, which suggests that Americans should adopt a more French way of life. But many stresses are doubtless unavoidable. Civilization does not rest easily on an animal that ran wild for so many generations. People who can take the characteristic pressures of the modern and (hypothetical) future environment—who can even thrive on them—have an obvious advantage and are likely to beget more than their share of children. It is possible that a whole series of technological cultures like ours must arise, disintegrate, and be painfully rebuilt before enough of the human race has developed the kind of personality needed for their maintenance. The same applies, perhaps, to most androdes.

So my guess is that the older races in the universe may have somewhat greater ability to visualize, imagine, and reason than we have, but if so, it is not overwhelmingly greater. Our highest intellects could talk to them and understand most of what they were doing, though we might never have thought of it for ourselves. However, by human standards, our elders are apt to be emotional giants, with a balance, an insight, a creativity, such as we can hardly imagine—but from which we could learn some sanity ourselves.

Chapter 8

On the Nature and Origin of Science

THE LAST CHAPTER went a little more into sheer speculation than is the aim of this book. Let us stick closer to home; our species will be in this neighborhood for a long time to come. Probably there are no races enormously advanced beyond us within many light-years, or they would have arrived here by now.

Of course, it is possible that we have been visited a million years or ten thousand years ago. There would be no record of it in either case. Or we may have been visited quite recently—we may be under constant surveillance—but for various reasons the elders do not wish us to know it. If one of these two rather implausible sentences reflects truth, it would not seem to make any immediate practical difference. We shall have to solve our own problems just the same.

Now, if, or when, we first go voyaging between the stars, we will not arrive surreptitiously. Any natives we find will know we have arrived. Elder species might conceal their presence to avoid distorting the natural evolution of local cultures by their own awesome example or from some other esoteric motive. But a young and bumptious race like man is most unlikely to take any such measures, especially when there is so much he can learn only by making direct contact with extra-Terrestrials. Presumably the same thing applies to most androdes at our own stage of cultural evolution. Any spaceships they may send to Earth will arrive with fanfare—which is rather good proof that none have arrived in historical times. (I shall not waste space on the "flying saucer" silliness.) Before they have the capability of making the trip in person, they should be able to signal. Are they doing so at this moment, hoping for a reply? Is an expedition on its way as you read this?

Such questions are answerable only by experience. But although we can say little about any specific stellar region, including our own, we can try to assess the likelihood in terms of galactic statistics. That is, we can imagine the *average* condition of androde species today that are about as old as ourselves. Even a hundred-year edge in scientific progress would make an enormous difference. How likely are we to be technologically outclassed by our evolutionary contemporaries? To estimate this, we must study the human past.

Surely all races begin in some equivalent of a stone age. Maybe other worlds have resources unknown to us, especially if they are nonterrestrial. But minerals must be universally available—also, we suppose, biological products analogous to wood, bone, shell, etc. Man went from this savagery to machine civilization in two major steps. First there was the neolithic revolution, in which such basic inventions as agriculture, the wheel, metallurgy, writing, and city life were made. Second was the development of science and the application of its findings to technology. It is hard to see how any androdes can go from hand axes to spaceships by an essentially different route. So the problem is whether they will actually do so.

The Genesis of Civilization

Man began on the first stage only about nine thousand years ago, which is no large fraction of the time he has existed. This fact, that he was a savage for many millenniums before he started being a farmer, indicates that the transition was not due to any ineluctable logic of events. Indeed, the evidence is that agriculture was at first a step backward. As the well-know anthropologist F. Bordes has pointed out to me,[1] the life of a paleolithic hunter was short but merry. Game was abundant, and cave excavations show the cultures were esthetically rich. It was probably the drying up of the Near East, the shrinking of forests and dwindling of wildlife that forced certain weak tribes to develop substitutes. What but desperation could have turned free woodsmen into wretched serfs? In such an economy it became possible for the few to exploit the many: hence kings, priests, scribes, and the dawn of civilization. But if the glaciers had not retreated northward so fast, trailing the rain belt behind them, we would most likely be pursuing the aurochs yet.

The circumstances that compel the invention of agriculture need not be the same for every planet, as far as we can tell. But it does look as if they are always rather special and difficult. Therefore I think savagery is more common than civilization in races of our age. To be sure, some few species may have taken the first step earlier in their existence than we did.

Once it has been taken, it seems irrevocable. Agricultural societies crowd out the hunters, if for no other reason than that a square mile planted in grain will support far more people than a square mile of wilderness. Moreover, the sedentary peoples (on Earth and I suppose everywhere) are more progressive in the beginning. So radical a change of life requires many adaptations. Early neolithic society was extremely inventive.

But eventually, technological progress slowed. Social stasis became an ideal. Some thinkers blame this on the invention of writing, which produced a class of priestly literates, a type that is notoriously conservative and soon gained tremendous influence. Now and then, over broad areas, there were actual setbacks, for example, the dark age that followed the post-Homeric invasion of the Mediterranean world by barbarians armed with iron weapons.

Advances were made, of course, but they were largely through the slow evolution of rule-of-thumb craftsmanship. And this can only go so far. It can develop a Renaissance caravel but not a clipper ship, most certainly not an airplane. A body of scientific knowledge must be acquired, or the race will forever depend on the limited energies of water, wind, fire, and muscle. The question before us now is whether this is an inevitable development. Granted that once the neolithic breakthrough has been made, a civilization at about the technological level of the Roman Empire is pretty sure to evolve in time, is a true science then bound to follow? I think not. Some peculiar social conditions are required. But to argue my case I must go rather far afield.[2]

The Nature of Science

Science cannot simply be defined as exact knowledge. In the first place, as the French mathematician Poincaré once remarked, a heap of unorganized facts is no more a science than a heap of bricks is a house. Furthermore, information that is both precise and highly organized need not be scientific. The classical Chinese scholar or the modern English professor knows just what he is talking about, but the subject matter is proudly nonscientific. Music and theology also come to mind. Even exact, systematic knowledge about the physical universe is not necessarily science. The Babylonians tabulated stellar and planetary motions with some precision, had pretty good mathematics to help them—and came up with astrology.

Clearly the goal and method of gathering facts are more important than the particular facts that happen to turn up at any given time. The scientific method is certainly not identical with the playful tinkering that doubtless led to the bow and arrow or with the painful learning from experience that produced agriculture. Conceivably a researcher could try everything in a shotgun fashion and eventually stumble on a discovery, but in practice he has no way to relate isolated observations to each other without a theory; and the same theory will suggest to him what else to look for and how to refine his knowledge of what he has already found.

Without trying to define what science "is"—something that no one has yet done to the satisfaction of practicing scientists—we can describe it as a body of more or less organized fact and theory together with a process of discovery involving hypothetical explanations whose deductive consequences are checked against observed data and that are discarded when they don't work. This is quite different from a collection of industrial recipes and gadgets. Science can indicate ways to make such things, but science is not itself a technology.

Accidental Factors in the Evolution of Science

Of course, society does not always know what it wants or pay attention to what is homely and unspectacular. As Campbell once pointed out, the cathode-ray tube of the 1870's was a laboratory toy because the primary interest of electrical researchers then was concentrated on motors and arc lights. Imagine that someone had started playing with that toy, had let the cathode radiation pass through a metal disk with a hole to make a bright spot on the anode, and had applied a charge to this disk. He would immediately have seen how the spot varied in size as he varied the charge. It would have been a natural next step to experiment with a grid of parallel wires, which in turn would have led almost inevitably to a triode amplifier. Radar might have been a reality in 1900. Progress in electronics, and hence in chemistry and nuclear physics, would have been speeded up fantastically.[3] However, this did not happen, chiefly because the contemporary world was demanding more efficient large-scale apparatus—not highly sensitive electronic responses on an exceedingly small scale.

There are many similar cases, also in theoretical science. Thus, the seventeenth-century physicist Christian Huygens advanced a particle concept of light that fell on stony ground, though it might have caused an early development of quantum mechanics. On the other hand, many happy accidents led to discoveries that could otherwise have waited for decades, for example radioactivity. One may well wonder how many potentialities we are neglecting today.

Admittedly the internal development of a given branch of science has a certain sequence. You cannot quantitatively justify heliocentric astronomy before you have a body of data like Tycho's, or visualize a galaxy before you know what a planetary system is. The inverse-square law of gravitation has small value without the calculus. But there is no obvious reason why the "human" sciences—psychology, sociology, anthropology, economics, and so on—could not be highly developed on a world with a very backward physical science. It is quite possible that the success of physics and chemistry has smothered those "human" sciences, partly by attracting talent from them and partly by imposing false canons on them. If the methods appropriate to the study of the atom are not well suited to the study of man (which seems plausible), then the physical-science orientation of the modern world has forced "human" science into an unnatural imitative mold, and its disappointing results can be understood.

The disappointment is not necessarily due to the greater complexity of the subject. Perhaps human phenomena would look less complex if we did not insist on trying to explain them in language of the physical sciences. From this viewpoint, Shakespeare would have been a great pioneer in the science of man, had that not been stillborn because the science of matter was developing so vigorously. But this is frankly speculative. Let us turn back to the evolution of science-as-we-know-it.

Very possibly society, rather than inherent complexity, is to blame for the fact that relativistic physics had to wait until the twentieth century for elucidation. The Indo-European languages base their structure on substantives and actions (nouns and verbs). They draw an unreal distinction between what a "thing" *is* and what it *does*, and compound this confusion by separating its qualities from the "thing" itself—as if "heaviness" had some existence apart from the class of heavy objects.

If in scientific theory there is reason to suppose that some action is taking place, a man who thinks in Indo-European terms finds it all too natural to imagine that there must be something that acts. Thus, classical physics had cause to believe in electromagnetic undulations, or strictly speaking, in certain phenomena describable by wave equations. It was therefore a linguistic (not a logical) necessity to postulate an "ether" that could undulate. This ether became more or less identified with absolute space. But the substantive concept of space and of time is due merely to the fact that in the Indo-European languages "space" and "time" are nouns.

Newton's contemporary Leibniz recognized the self-contradictory character of "absolute space," as is shown by his correspondence with Newton's pupil and advocate Samuel Clarke. He pointed out that the only way to detect it would be to find something that was absolutely at rest—but this particle or ether or what-have-you would, by the definition of motion, be moving with respect to everything else! His suggestions lay fallow to Poincaré's day, and not before Einstein did anyone base a complete physical theory on the insight. This is not a matter of Leibniz' being an obscure figure like Mendel. Is it too much to suggest that his acute analysis was neglected because the structure of Western language made it difficult to understand?

Without such a handicap Newton and his successors might well have created a theory of relativity. It would probably have looked more like E. A. Milne's than Einstein's but would have reached many of the same conclusions, and I daresay it would have stimulated an earlier development of non-Euclidean geometry and quantum mechanics. Atomic energy in the eighteenth or nineteenth century? Why not?

In some respects, though, we have been linguistically fortunate. However imperfectly, our languages do reflect enough of the structure of the universe for us to think in scientific terms. It is probably more than chance that the Chinese, for all their high civilization, never developed a true science but remained—from the modern point of view—tinkerers; or that Oriental scientists today usually write in some European language.

The Genesis of the Scientific Method

Even granted a suitable tongue, science is not inevitable. Some people would call it a natural development, derived from prehistoric gropings. In this view, the first man to observe the Sun's path through the year was the first astronomer, and so on. When they get into recorder history, these thinkers see science continuing to evolve through Egyptian surveyors, Babylonian astrologers, Greek philosophers, Roman engineers, and medieval alchemists. They make the scientific method proper only the latest link in a very cold chain.

But I myself think that although accumulated knowledge was certainly necessary for science to originate, it was not sufficient. We have always had observation, cataloguing, accidental discovery, practical improvement of practical techniques, but I repeat that these are not science. All the tinkering and all the philosophical speculations in the world will never yield the theory of electromagnetism, nor the electronics based on this theory. So, if we cannot find a particular date to label "Birth of Science," we can at least narrow the event down to a small group of people within a short span of time who took the first step beyond tinkering and speculation. Since European man alone possessed the scientific method a few centuries ago, and everyone else has learned it from him, we need only ask whether he actually invented it or merely improved what he had borrowed from someone else.

One school of thought credits the Arabs of the Middle Ages with being the fathers of science. It is true that they were a more educated people than their European contemporaries and that they not only possessed a great deal of information handed down from the Greeks and Hindus but did some independent work. Examples such as Alhazen's treatise on optics in the eleventh century, and the work of others in astronomy, chemistry, and medicine, do suggest that they were on the verge of a scientific revolution. But it never materialized. Scholarship fell back to arid controversies much like those of the late medieval Schoolmen. Perhaps the religious fanaticism of the Seljuks and the Crusade period that it provoked was responsible.

The fact is that Europe took very little protoscience from outside sources. Except for occasional ideas like zero (indispensable) and alchemy (a blind alley that wasted many talented man-years and contributed nothing except a bit of laboratory technique), post-Roman Western thought is nearly independent of foreign influences—as far as science goes. We certainly learned much else from Africa and the Orient.

The most conventional reconstruction traces the scientific method back to the Greeks, asserting that it existed in Hellenistic times and was revived in the Renaissance. But with all due respect for the Classical world, this is simply not true. The Hellenistic era did come amazingly close to such a revolution, both intellectual and industrial. Hero's aeolipile was an embryonic steam turbine. Archimedes appreciated the potentialities of mathematics and machinery alike. A number of automata were invented, chiefly for stage effects in temples, and more important devices such as the water wheel. In the area of basic knowledge, there was endless hypothesizing about the nature of things, much solid mathematical work, and valuable observations in fields like astronomy, physics, taxonomy, biology, and sociology. The point is that all this remained the province of the philosopher. (I should perhaps make a small exception for medicine, which by Galen's time was on the verge of becoming truly scientific—but this petered out.) On the one hand the Greeks had rules of logic and a body of theory, on the other hand a good deal of empirical data and useful technique. But the two were never joined, and it is this blending of analysis, hypothesis, and experiment that constitutes science.

No natural law forbade the event in Hellenistic times. Though the Greeks suffered from certain deficiencies, such as the lack of good optical glass, this could have been overcome. They must have noticed the magnifying effect of a sphere of glass, and a few years of work ought to have produced a decent lens. The need for such a lens could have occurred to any physician or jeweler. Even without making up these lacks, the Hellenistic world could have performed most of Galileo's and Newton's experiments, such as those with pendulums and falling bodies. To get very far in these lines they would have needed a mechanical clock, but that had already been adumbrated.

Why, then, did they fail to create a science?

Technical deficiencies must be a partial answer. Since there were no lenses to start with, Jan Lippershey's accidental invention of the telescope was not possible. Though communications were not much worse than in the Renaissance, there was no printing press, which made it harder to establish a universal community of scholarship. But troubles like these were not insuperable and do not explain the failure to conduct methodical experiments with the apparatus available.

It was not lack of intellectual enterprise. The Greek thinkers were men of enormous curiosity and ingenuity. But this intellect was faced in another direction from that of the Western society succeeding Rome. Experiment was not respectable. The goal was pure knowledge, independent of the senses and of any merely practical application. No philosophy was considered to need empirical proof. Even Hero and Archimedes were rather apologetic about their own material accomplishments, and they never attracted many disciples.

These are purely social phenomena, perhaps due to large slave populations. Manual labor, even the most skilled, was not fit for the Hellenistic intellectual, only for slaves and artisans. The plentiful supply of cheap hands not only made such work socially degrading but left small inducement to create new machines. In our culture, engineering problems have often instigated pure research, for example, in thermodynamics. But few engineering problems in Classical times drew the notice of first-rate minds. (A similar attitude prevailed in the heyday of Spain, and it is interesting to note how seldom Spaniards have made important contributions to science, despite the ample talent they have shown in other endeavors.)

When Classical civilization collapsed, the so-called Dark Ages set in. To some degree this is a misnomer. Though politically chaotic, the period was one of great technological advance. Major innovations like the horse collar, the horseshoe, the mold-board plow, and the deep-water ship were made—all this in the "Dark Ages" proper, say, prior to the Hildebrandine Papacy. Thus a preoccupation with mechanics has characterized Western society from its very birth, an attitude that other cultures, like the Byzantine, found rather repugnant.[4] The reason is obscure. Maybe it was the result of the Germanic barbarians, who had not had time to develop snobbishness about work or trade, being suddenly confronted with the technology, the complicated problems, and the acute labor shortage of the dying Empire.

Technological improvement continued at an accelerating pace through the high Middle Ages, roughly 1050–1450. At this time the intellectual foundations of the present world were also being laid. One cannot build a Gothic cathedral or trade across continents without having a considerable body of precise knowledge. Meanwhile the ideas of Plato and Aristotle were not simply parroted but adapted and extended in the universities.

By the time of the Renaissance, gunpowder, clocks, the magnetic compass, clear glass, automatic machinery like water mills, and much else had become commonplace. So too, and far more importantly, had the habit of wondering what the world was actually like, rather than what it ought to be like. Galileo did not spring from nowhere. Some of his father's writings, remarking on the foolishness of those who blindly accept authority, are extant. They reflect a climate of opinion that men like Robert Grosseteste and Roger Bacon had heralded centuries earlier. Not only had the working engineer of the Renaissance reached a level that would have astonished his Roman ancestors, but the philosopher was considering that same world in which the engineer operated. And engineer and philosopher respected each other. They were often identical.

We cannot be entirely sure what brought about this situation. The long-standing social acceptability of trade and handicraft must have been important. The capitalist—and the Middle Ages had capitalists on a grand scale—will naturally be interested in useful discoveries and support the men who can make them. This attitude will in turn influence the clergy, the aristocracy, and the military if these are as close to the mercantile class as they normally have been in Europe. For instance, a systematic interest in astronomy might have originated with the navigators of the fifteenth and sixteenth centuries, to whom exact knowledge of the heavens was important. A more recent example would be Count Rumford's spadework on the conservation of energy, based on a study of the industrial process of boring cannon. Generally speaking, the expansion of trade and industry has given both pure and applied science a continual stimulus in the form of challenging new problems.

But a logical, analytic approach is just as necessary as an empirical one. The development of this thought pattern may perhaps be traced back to the scholars and theologians of the Middle Ages. The tolerant Classical world could let any number of different philosophies flourish, but Christendom required unanimity. This led to fierce competition between rival schools of thought, which in turn forced the development of sharp intellectual tools. The Judeo-Christian tradition also discouraged the fuzzy subjectivism of Asia, insisting that the nature of the world is independent of man but discoverable by him.

To summarize, the scientific method appears to have been born in the later European Renaissance after a gestation extending far back into the Middle Ages. Its ancestry is not quite certain but may well consist largely of this triad: accumulated technology, Christian respect for order and theory, and a vigorous practical-minded capitalism. Whether this be right or wrong, it seems clear that science was not a matter of inevitable progress but of the accidentally right combination of social circumstances—and the course of its development has also frequently been determined by accident. Nor do we have any guarantee that it will continue. Social conditions may change so radically that scientists become as extinct as Osiris worshippers.

Altogether, then, I think that our present level of scientific-technological development is somewhat improbable. We are ahead of the average for our age group. Doubtless we are not in the very forefront. Someone else can have been luckier than we. And, too, the androdes who have existed longer than man have had more opportunity for the critical accidents to happen.

Still, I suspect man is among the leaders in the outer parts of the galaxy, where the young and middle-aged stars occur. But the stars' number is tremendous. If there are billions of sentient races, there should be millions, at the very least, whose knowledge is comparable to ours. Some of them may lie within communication range. What are our chances of ever getting in touch with them?

Chapter 9

Voices from the Stars

AN INSTRUMENT that might have been framed in steel by Brobdingnagian spiders turns a face the size of a football field skyward and listens. A man watches a trace on a fluorescent screen, scrawled by stars and galaxies and the clouds that fill the cosmos. Somewhere else a computer chatters, reeling out numbers that will be points on a new map of space and time. And still there are those who say romance is dead.

Radio astronomy was begotten a generation ago, when Karl Jansky first showed that the strange dry hiss in his receivers originated beyond the Solar System. But the science lay in embryo until after World War II. Then revolutionary electronic techniques brought it to birth. Now it is opening fresh vistas almost daily. These waves can penetrate where visible light does not go, through our murky atmosphere or the light-years-thick dust banks in space. And they carry unique information. The interstellar medium does not glow, but it sings in the radio frequencies; the radio spectrum of any object is as revealing as the rainbow it makes through a prism. We are like men suddenly given a whole extra sense.

The promise of such astronomy has lured a large number of instruments into being. Radio telescopes, they are called, and because the wave lengths they detect are long, they must themselves be large to have reasonably good definition—so that their users can say, "Such-and-such a thing is emitting in such-and-such a part of the sky," rather than, "Something whose shape we don't know is emitting in an area we can't pin down." The United States National Radio Astronomy Observatory near Greenbank, West Virginia, has a telescope eighty-five feet across. The largest in the world is the two-hundred-fifty-footer maintained at Jodrell Bank in England by the University of Manchester. The United States Navy began construction of a receiver whose dish was to be more than six hundred feet wide, near Sugar Grove, West Virginia. Unfortunately, this project has been discontinued. For reasons that will become apparent, I think its importance so great that it should be resumed as soon as possible.

But if these instruments can detect radiation that has come multiple millions of light-years, can they not detect less powerful sources closer to us? And may these not include beams from other stars, modulated by intelligent life?

Even before Marconi transmitted across the Atlantic, the dream arose of calling to another planet. Around 1900 the Prix Guzman was founded in Paris—a hundred thousand francs, which was then a goodly sum, for the first person to establish interplanetary communication. But Mars was excluded as being too easy! In spite of this, the red world was the target of several attempts at radio contact. Now we feel pessimistic about finding any races comparable to ourselves in the Solar System—maybe too pessimistic—but are more sanguine about finding them elsewhere than we were in the past. No doubt someone will try an interstellar signal in the near future: within a century, probably less. Or if we blow up our civilization before that time, we ought to have successors who will try. An extra thousand years to wait is negligible on the galactic time scale.

But this implies that others may be trying to call us. And today we have highly sensitive receivers. It is simple to listen for any possible messages. Or is it?

Project Ozma

The first serious analysis of the problem that I know of was by Giuseppe Cocconi and Philip Morrison in 1959.[1] They pointed out several requirements for an interstellar beam. The frequencies used should not be too much absorbed by dust and gas in space or by the atmospheres of hypothetical target planets. They should not require unduly great power or complicated techniques at the source. Naturally, this is a relative matter. A more advanced civilization than ours may well do with ease what would be difficult or impossible for us. But the senders must bear in mind that whoever receives the signal may not be so adept. Therefore the frequencies should be fairly easy to detect. These criteria are met by the band from approximately one to ten thousand megacycles per second. A more recent and detailed calculation by Frank Drake of the National Radio Astronomy Observatory raises the desirable lower frequency to about a thousand megacycles, though if signals are sent and intended to be received above atmospheres, the upper limit is as high as thirty thousand megacycles.[2]

This still leaves a tremendously wide spectrum. Searching it wave length by wave length, in every part of the sky, would take an appalling amount of time, during which valuable instruments would be tied up that might be employed on fruitful projects. But the senders must realize this, and so choose a wave length that they think will occur to anyone capable of detecting it. Cocconi and Morrison suggest the frequency 1,420 megacycles, the twenty-one-centimeter line continuously emitted by neutral interstellar hydrogen.

One might reasonably ask if a signal would not get unnoticeably faint as it crosses the gulfs between the stars. But the case is not actually so bad. Of course no one is broadcasting to the whole galaxy. We might be able to pick up broadcasts from the nearer stars but surely not beyond our immediate neighborhood. However, a tight beam fades much more slowly than a spherical wave front. The diameter of the radio mirror at the source, which focuses the beam, is important. Cocconi and Morrison calculate that if we used a mirror the size of the one at Jodrell Bank, it would strain our technical resources to send an impulse that equals the galactic background noise ten light-years away. But with something like the proposed Sugar Grove instrument we could today send an identifiable signal considerably farther. There is no reason in principle why such transmissions cannot be made across thousands of light-years.

Of course, it is desirable to avoid the galactic background as far as possible. If we begin by aiming our telescopes at stars lying well off the Milky Way plane, the interference can be reduced as much as forty times. This in turn extends the range over which we can listen and thus the probability of hearing something. If we have no luck in those directions, it will be time enough to try the noisier central plane, which does offer some compensation in holding so many more stars.

The twenty-one-centimeter wave length is not the only one worth trying. Sebastian von Hoerner points out that galactic interference is much less if we use just twice this frequency—a stunt so obvious as to be considered by any androde planning to signal. On grounds of economy in transmission, Drake makes the three-centimeter wave length another good bet.[8] No doubt reasons can be found for tuning in several others. Once an initial contact has been made, some highly sophisticated questions of the optimum channel for detailed communication will arise.

Besides these questions of wave length, band width, and interference, there is the matter of Doppler shift. If a source of undulant energy is moving, the frequencies it emits ahead of itself are increased while those that it emits backward are decreased. (The same principle makes a train whistle sound shriller as it nears, deeper as it goes away.) Whether the interstellar signal comes from a natural globe or an artificial satellite, there is bound to be relative motion between it and us, constantly changing at that. But the difficulty can be overcome by making due allowance for the uncertainties involved. And if we ever actually receive a message, Doppler shift will give us valuable information, for example, what kind of orbit the source has.

All in all, the prospect looks so good—at least in relation to the small initial investment of time and skilled manpower—that official attempts were made under Drake's direction as part of the general testing and development of techniques. This by now famous program was dubbed Project Ozma. A focusing on the stars Tau Ceti and Epsilon Eridani gave a negative result. This does not rule them out, since the detection equipment may not have been sufficiently sensitive and all the easily imaginable bands were not tried. Part of the time of the six-hundred-foot telescope was to have been devoted to such listening. This alone seems to me to justify the completion of that instrument.

The Likelihood of Success

Although I have argued that red dwarf stars are just about as likely to have inhabited planets as are any other kind, it is certainly reasonable to try first those suns that are not too different from ours. They are few in our neighborhood. Su-Shu Huang admits only two: Epsilon Eridani, type K2, luminosity 0.34 Sol, distance 10.8 light-years; and Tau Ceti, type G4, luminosity 0.38 Sol, distance 11.8 light-years.[4] Cocconi and Morrison also name these, plus 0_2 Eridani and Epsilon Indi, as local rough approximations of Sol in directions where the galactic interference is low. All happen to be southern stars, which emphasizes the need of at least two really big instruments for a future Project Ozma, one in each hemisphere. In addition, Cocconi and Morrison list Alpha Centauri, 70 Ophiuchi, and 61 Cygni as candidates, which, however, lie near the Milky Way plane. We recall that the last two of these have been shown to possess superjovian planets, which makes the chance of bodies about the size of Earth look fairly good. Alpha Centauri is our nearest neighbor, 4.3 light-years away. It is a double star (with a faint red third partner, Proxima, at a considerable distance) whose brightest member is very like Sol. But since the two main suns average only some twenty A.U. distant, on a highly eccentric orbit, the likelihood of a terrestrial world is not great.

Discouraging though this may sound, we can take heart from the fact that within fifty light-years there are approximately a hundred appropriate objects, that is, main-sequence dwarfs roughly between G0 and K2 with visual magnitudes less than +6. The same region contains far more stars that a conservative regards as unsuitable but that I, for one, think should be tried after the less controversial possibilities are exhausted.

There is no way to predict the odds for or against success. They depend on how many races are at this moment making an attempt to call someone else. We specifically, the Solar System, will no doubt be the target if the callers live fairly close by. But we also have a small chance of intercepting a message aimed at some other star and a perhaps greater chance of detecting a beam from very far away that has systematically been sweeping its own sky.

I have suggested that although intelligent life is quite common, scientifically oriented machine civilizations like ours are probably rare, especially out here on the galactic fringe. We would be fortunate indeed to make contact with anyone just a few light-years off. A more elaborate analysis by von Hoerner points out that the longevity of such cultures is also an important factor. The race that has gotten to the point of transmitting interstellar signals could destroy itself, or degenerate physically or mentally, or lose interest in science. His mathematical treatment leads him to think that the likelihood of any given star sending at any given time is slight. Therefore the chances are that whatever signals we receive will come from far off, on the order of a thousand light-years or more.[5]

Interesting though his essay is, it depends frankly on giving arbitrary numerical values to such quantities as the probability that an average race will destroy itself once it has a machine civilization. Von Hoerner sets these values higher than I would —except for the probability that a scientifically oriented culture will last indefinitely. This he considers to be nil. I am not so sure. We have no reason to suppose that every intelligent species must have just that blend of instincts and go through just that course of history which have brought man to his present peril. For that matter, we have no proof that our own scientific state of mind is doomed, in this or any future century. It may be so, but we are rash to claim that it must be so.

Interstellar Communication

Nonetheless, if we are to be serious about contacting other races, we must eventually build instruments that can detect signals from extremely far away, and use them to scan the sky continuously. This operation can be automated, and Arthur Clarke has suggested that a good location for it might be the far side of the Moon. The Lunar mass should screen out interference from Terrestrial sources and, during the two-week night, the Sun.

A race that was trying to make initial contact across very great distances would not aim at us, or at anyone, especially. Sol is a most inconspicuous object in that swarm of similar stars enclosed by a sphere a thousand light-years in radius. Rather, the seekers would steadily sweep the sky with a great many beams, back and forth. When an answering signal was received, a beam could be directed at its source. In time we shall also have to carry out a search like that. Someone out there may be waiting to hear, and unwilling to transmit before they do. Even those who are sending out probe signals may not get around to our part of the heavens for a long time if they don't hear anything from us.

Once contact is established, there will be some formidable problems of communication. Years must pass between message and reply, possibly centuries. To begin with, there will be no common language whatsoever. Nevertheless, rational intercourse is possible.

The first signals must be something that is plainly not of natural origin. One would expect the wave to be pulse modulated and to carry some identifying information. It might, for example, run through a series of small prime numbers, representing them by bursts; or it might reiterate some arithmetical sums. But this will scarcely be all. The senders cannot wish to spend decades in getting a mere acknowledgment. It would be best to start right in on the work of building a mutual code. So the first signal ought to run through a long cycle, taking months or years before it repeats itself. (And listeners, who will probably "come in in the middle," must allow for that.) Beginning with mathematics, it can develop a basic language.

To see how, let us picture a few elementary lessons. Compare these dot-and-dash messages:

```
•   – •  •– ••
••  – •• •– ••••
••• – •• •– •••••
```

Obviously these are sums, with – standing for "plus" and •– standing for "equals." In this manner, by progressing through many stages of increasing complication, a sophisticated mathematical vocabulary can be explained.

Now let us send a dot followed by some code symbol, two dots followed by another symbol, etc. These new symbols may at first be taken for the names of the numbers. But if then we send two of the symbols that substitute for single dots, the – that means "added to," one of the symbols that substitute for eight dots, a fresh symbol, and still another new symbol, we are representing a chemical reaction: two atoms of Element 1 (hydrogen) plus one atom of Element 8 (oxygen) yields a molecule of water. Our listeners should not require many examples before they get the idea. Thus we give names to the chemical elements, processes like combination, and compounds like water. Through such paradigms, a physical science vocabulary is built up.

There are considerable difficulties in the way of interstellar television, but crude pictures might be sent even in the initial stages. This could be done simply by specifying mathematically a great many points on a co-ordinate grid. When the listeners draw these points on a sheet of paper (or whatever they use) they will find that the dots make a picture. The method is too slow and clumsy to employ very often, but it should excite enough interest at the receiving end that the listeners would become willing to erect the great apparatus that can handle the band width needed for television.

The reply to the first cosmic signal should be equally carefully planned, and run through as long a cycle. Having already been given the beginnings of a code, the second race can develop it further in the course of sending information that is new to the first race. Thus a reasonably complete language can slowly be worked out—a different one between every pair of worlds, though all that are used by one particular world will be related. Though conversation as we understand it is impossible, even over the shortest of interstellar distances, discourse is not.

Time Scales

Plainly, the greater the separation of the two stars, the longer must be the wait between signal and reply. If we had responded to a call across a thousand light-years in the time of Christ, we would only now be getting an answer in our turn. But it is not fantastic to believe that we would keep the tradition alive so long, through all the vicissitudes of our history. Christians have awaited the Second Coming for an equal time and are quite prepared to await it indefinitely. The expectation of such a message might prove to be a civilizing factor, or at least one that helps keep alive the scientific state of mind.

In fact, as von Hoerner remarks, a feedback effect should occur. If a race calls and calls for centuries, unavailingly, their interest in the project may be expected to decline. On the other hand, success will stimulate fresh efforts. He concludes that there are two possibilities, either of which has a reasonable chance of being realized: a considerable amount of communication activity between long-lived civilizations that are fairly close to each other (less than a thousand light-years); or little or no exchange at greater distances between more short-lived societies. He feels that the intermediate case, of some but not much communication, is too unstable to be at all likely.

I myself think that a fairly large amount of communication —between several per cent of all the stars there are—is more probable than none at all and that a small amount is not so hard to maintain as von Hoerner estimates. He himself suggests that once a contact has been made, the effort will tend to persist and to expand through space, especially among older and presumably more sensible species than man, who really can plan in terms of millenniums. One would expect the race that first calls to be more advanced than the race that first receives, and thus to act as a teacher, not only of science and technology, but perhaps of moral and political lessons it has learned in its own past. The receiving race will almost surely transmit in its turn, eventually contacting still others and bringing them into the general fellowship.

Even if I am right in guessing that savages are more common than scientists, this need not bar the spread of communication. Although the proportion of scientific cultures is low, their absolute number must be quite high. So they should not normally be too far apart to get in touch by radio.

As for discouragement, I think von Hoerner exaggerates its importance. True, we cannot easily imagine human beings manning interstellar transmitters for century after century if there is no result. But we do not expect them to do so in the first place. The signals will be sent out automatically, probably from extra-terrestrial installations. The equipment can be Solar-powered and self-servicing, requiring virtually no attention. In short, once the radio search is well under way, it will continue of itself for an exceedingly long time. Similar considerations should apply to any androdes making the same attempt. For these reasons, I think that even sparse communication represents a stable condition that can exist through large parts of the outer galaxy. Closer to the nucleus, where stars are older and more crowded, I think there must be a great deal of talk going on.

It is hardly necessary to tell any reader of this book why the effort is worth while, even if it proves fruitless for centuries to come. Success will be among the most important events of human history. The exchange of scientific and technological information is a dazzling enough prospect. The other beings are perhaps ahead of us in all respects, in which case we can advance our own development tremendously just by listening to them. Even if they are, on the whole, merely comparable to us, we shall have much to learn. I have already tried to show the irregular and accidental character of scientific advance, which suggests that any two like-minded species could fill in gaps in each other's knowledge. There is most certainly one area in which each has a treasure hoard of information that the other lacks: its own planet and the life thereon. Think what it would mean to us to receive a complete description of an extra-Terrestrial biology.

But all this looks nearly trivial when we consider the intangibles. Each world out there can offer us an entire new set of histories, arts, philosophies, beliefs, and modes of living. Some are no doubt of strictly academic interest to us, but others should enter our consciousness like a flame. We need only hark back to the most brilliant periods of Earth's past to see how vital the cross-fertilization of different societies has been.

And today that element is dying out of our existence. Machine civilization, irresistibly powerful, spreads across Earth and devours all others. Differences remain between countries, but they narrow with every generation. We see before us the specter of a planet-wide empire, perhaps not calling itself that, perhaps not unified in name, but as rigid as Pharaonic Egypt, and with no outsiders to break its paralyzing grip. It need not even be a slave state; the individual may have numerous liberties. But if there is nothing he can do with it, his freedom is empty. Already today we feel the first gnawings of that millennial hollowness. Yet we move on toward the empire, for our alternative is to renounce the machine.

The newness that is our salvation may come from the stars.

Chapter 10

Tomorrow's Argosies

FOR ALL ITS WONDERFUL POTENTIALITIES, interstellar radio communication is under severe handicaps. Besides that maddening time lag, the knowledge it bestows is secondhand and the experience it represents is vicarious. It can still widen our mental horizons more than we can now guess. Yet we are animals, who through most of our existence have tracked down our own quarry. A scientist may spend a happy lifetime unraveling the implications of a message from Tau Ceti, but most young men would infinitely rather go there in person.

Besides, we cannot be sure that any Project Ozma will ever work out. We may lie beyond the effective range of whoever is transmitting. In any case, other intelligent races also have something to teach us. Quite apart from the discoveries and the inspiration that would come from exploring inhabited planets, these beings might often have skills that we do not possess, for example, in biology. More important than their technical tricks are the intangibles mentioned in the last chapter. We would not like our nonhuman acquaintances forever limited to those that happen to possess radios.

Already today, when man has not yet set foot on the Moon, we look at the stars with a certain hunger. It is bound to grow once the Solar System has become familiar to us. Can it ever be appeased?

At first glance any sensible person will exclaim, "Certainly not!" Interstellar distances belong to another order of magnitude than interplanetary. At the high speed of a hundred miles per second, which we have no immediate prospect of even approaching, we could reach Mars in days, but it would take eight thousand years to reach Alpha Centauri. The average time between local stars would be nearly twice as great as that.

The Hyperdrive

As far as we know today, light travels at the ultimate possible velocity, and it still needs years to go from sun to sun. On this account, fiction writers—including me—who wish to deal with extra-Solar travel usually assume that there is some way of getting around this law of physics. We know very well that you cannot simply accelerate a ship until it passes the speed of light. But may there not be aspects of the universe, still waiting to be discovered, that would permit us to get from here to there by some other means than ordinary acceleration?

To revive a hackneyed analogy, consider a sheet of paper. A bug at one corner wishes to go to the opposite corner. He need not cross the whole sheet if you will obligingly fold the paper around, so that the two corners lie next to each other. Instead, he can make in one step that journey that would have taken him hundreds of steps on a flat sheet. Does three-dimensional space have folds of which we can take corresponding advantage?

The analogy is actually false. The bug is not a two-dimensional inhabitant of the paper surface, but a three-dimensional creature that happens to be walking upon it. If it is folded, he goes from corner to corner by stepping off the surface with the help of a push exerted by his legs at right angles to it. But we *are* embedded in our space. Even if there are tucks in it, how can we generate a force perpendicular to all three of our space axes so as to enter those tucks?

Other methods have been fictionally postulated. There may be "holes" or "tunnels" in space. It may be possible to make a very large number of small quantum jumps per second. If, as Ernst Mach's analysis of mechanical principles suggests, inertia is an inductive effect, produced in matter by the gravitational field of the universe, then perhaps a ship can be isolated from this field during its journey and so offer no resistance to acceleration. I could go on multiplying examples of rather bad physics, but these will serve. Let us lump all such imaginary faster-than-light systems together as "hyperdrives."

We cannot say that one of them will never be invented.

That would be tantamount to saying we have discovered all the basic laws of nature. But we can say that we have no evidence for any laws that would permit a hyperdrive, and there are good reasons—not only in experimental science but in logic—to doubt their existence.

The fact that we have never been visited from outer space is not one of those reasons. As I remarked before, we may indeed have been, and not know it. But the sheer size of the galaxy is enough to account for our isolation. Imagine an androde race that invents a hyperdrive and sets out to explore all the planets in existence. Imagine them mounting so vast an effort that they complete a survey of fifty stars a year, almost one a week. (This implies more than giving each one a casual glance and passing on, an utterly pointless thing to do. I cannot emphasize too often that every planet is a world illimitably complex and various.) It will take them at least two billion years to finish exploring this galaxy—if it holds still. But of course a fraction of that time is enough to transform each planet completely. The job would be never-ending. I doubt if they would ever get around to giving this thin fringe where we are more than a cursory astronomical mapping.

The same problem of size makes ludicrous all thought of a galactic government. A mere thousand systems look far too cumbersome to allow a union. And I cannot see why anyone would desire to unify them. The immense diversity of environments, races, and viewpoints in such a region argues against any common purpose. Given a hyperdrive, it is not impossible that there are occasional Norman-like interstellar conquerors, whose aggressions cause alliances to be formed against them. But even on the largest feasible scale, such activity can occupy only a minute part of the entire galaxy. And it looks improbable in any event. What value has an uncolonizable planet to imperialists? Even worlds whose biochemistry happens to be enough like home that they can be settled will not solve any population problems, as the history of Europe vis-à-vis America testifies. In short, special circumstances may produce sporadic wars and political combinations; but if so, these are highly localized.

Peaceful intercourse like trade and cultural exchange seems

far more plausible. But this must also be limited. It cannot take place between races unless they are willing and able to engage in it, and do not live too far apart. Chance probably decides whether this is the case in any given sector.

I therefore imagine the long-run consequence of a hyperdrive as not one galactic civilization but widely scattered clusters of civilizations. Within each cluster there are several races that have some dealings with each other and many that are not concerned, being ignored or aloof. From time to time explorers, daring traders, missionaries, refugees, or other adventurous types make a long jump in search of new territory. Where they find fertile ground, planets that are useful and natives that are receptive to them, a new cluster is begun. Contact between clusters is very tenuous and, in almost every case, unofficial. Near the galactic nucleus, where the stars are closer together and many dwellers are anciently established, conditions may not be quite this anarchic; but even there I should think that any interstellar organization is loose and spatially limited.

Maybe several kinds of clusters exist in galactic space, their histories independent. For instance, the hydrogen and oxygen breathers can have little to trade with each other and perhaps little to say to each other once some scientific questions have been answered. But this gets us far out on the windy limb of speculation.

For that matter, the hyperdrive itself is rather airy. I only wanted to develop the idea a little to show what a hyperdrive cannot do. It can open the galaxy to human exploration, which will produce an era even more adventurous and intellectually revolutionary than the era that followed Columbus. No doubt it can find us planets to colonize. This will be good for the colonists but will make little or no economic difference to the mother world. A technology that can send fleets to the stars will not depend on them to return with food or textiles. Commerce will deal mostly in luxuries and curiosa. A hyperdrive cannot lead to a galactic imperium; nor can we ever really chart this one galaxy with its help, let alone the entire universe.

Certainly I wish that a faster-than-light engine will one day be invented or brought to us by outside visitors. But the odds against it look overwhelming. I shall therefore give the idea no further attention in this book but instead inquire whether it is possible to reach the stars using known principles of physics.

A Slow Boat to Centauri

The reaction drive, loosely called the rocket, does enable us to cross space. The energy we can get from chemical fuels is altogether insufficient to build up those speeds that are necessary to make extra-Solar crossings in anything like historical time. But atomic energy is another matter. Though it is not infinite either, it does amount to eighteen hundred million million foot-pounds per ounce of converted matter. If we ever find a way to produce—and control—this complete transformation, we will have fantastic powers at our fingertips. Even if we do not, but must continue to rely on atomic transmutation processes that are less than 1 per cent efficient, the case is hopeful.

Already developmental work is being done on the so-called ion jet. This device will use a fission reactor as the ultimate power source. An electrical system will ionize matter and eject it rearward. The jet will only work in space, but large ships assembled in orbit are contemplated. Although it will not furnish much thrust, the thrust can be continuous for weeks or months, so that high velocities are built up.

I do not feel at all reckless in predicting that a system like this can be greatly improved. Controlled hydrogen fusion should eventually replace the fission of heavy atoms as an energy source. The faster the rate at which matter is expelled, the less mass is needed to give the ship any particular velocity. Today, in the laboratory, protons or helium nuclei can be accelerated to nearly the speed of light. The engineers of the future should be able to project much denser beams at, say, half this speed. In that case (a jet, or exhaust, velocity one-half that of light) a ship needs a mass ratio of about 1.5 to reach one-tenth the velocity of light itself, allowing for deceleration at journey's end. This means that for every ton of ship and payload you wish to send to another star, you must expel half a ton of matter. If the system is to have a mass of ten thousand tons at journey's end, it must have a mass of fifteen thousand tons when it starts out.

An increased exhaust velocity reduces this requirement. If you eject radiation itself, the mass ratio needed to reach one-tenth light speed (and brake) is only about 1.2. It costs you two thousand tons to send ten thousand tons to another star. Of course, if you wish to travel faster, you must pay correspondingly more. In fact, the mass ratio is an exponential function of the maximum speed you plan to reach.

But let us keep it specific and imagine a ship—or more likely a small fleet—bound for Alpha Centauri at one-tenth light speed, 18,627 miles per second. Considering the mass ratios with which present-day rocketeers deal, this does not look physically unreasonable. But the trip will take more than forty-three years. Is that not too great a barrier?

It is not if social conditions are right. There can be so high a spirit of adventure that many will volunteer to embark with their families on a voyage from which only their children and grandchildren return. Such people are alive even today, even in this complacent America. Alternatively, a harsh government may sentence political offenders to go. They will have small choice in the matter, and can hope that their descendants will come home to such honor (or to such a changed world) that old scores are forgotten. Even if not officially exiled, some people may go just to get away from conditions on Earth that they dislike. There are precedents in history.

The ships will have to be self-supporting, but that is entirely possible. By recycling all organic matter, by growing green plants or algae in tanks under sun lamps, and by other similar methods the voyagers can live indefinitely in space. Means like this will already have been perfected in the Solar System, where scientists will have spent years at a time on hostile planets. Hazards like radiation can also be guarded against. After acceleration ceases, artificial gravity can be provided by rotating the ship about an axis long enough that the variation in centrifugal force is too small to produce dizziness.

The psychological dangers are worse. Cooped in a hull—even though it is a very big hull—for forty-three years, men and women will need to be highly compatible and have a great deal of self-discipline. They will need work that is so interesting they do not find the monotony unbearable. This suggests that artists, theoretical scientists, philosophers, and other high-level intellectuals are better crew material than the brawny heroes of fiction. Much work on the ships can possibly be done en route, thus furnishing occupation for the more down-to-earth types. There should be libraries, theaters, and gymnasiums. There should be gardens and perhaps a park area. The problems of sex and child rearing are obvious but soluble. And those who are born on the voyage may well grow up finding the ships entirely congenial.

I do not claim that just anyone could survive this trip. On the contrary, for most people it would spell madness and murder. But the human race is so various that I feel sure there are individuals who can stand such conditions and even thrive on them. This is the more plausible when we consider what help they should be able to get from the powerful emotion-regulating drugs of the future.

Having reached the Alpha Centauri system and explored for some years, the travelers will presumably want to come home. If they carried enough reaction mass from the start, they can simply re-enter their gigantic vessels and begin acceleration. (These mother ships, too big and fragile to land anywhere, will have remained in orbit while the crews traveled about in small sturdy spaceboats capable of setting down on planets.) But it seems more practical to get the reaction mass where they are. It may be water from a terrestrial world's lakes, or hydrogen from a jovian atmosphere, or something else; in any case, the equipment for obtaining and refining it should be less heavy and bulky than the mass itself.

Of course, this assumes that Alpha Centauri has planets that can furnish the necessary materials. But as great an enterprise as this would not be launched blindly. An unmanned, instrumented probe would have gone first. Being lighter, it travels faster and can reach the system and radio back enough data for men to decide whether an expedition is feasible. For that matter, the human travelers will no doubt send radio reports to Earth.

One may well speculate on how they will like man's home planet when they get back. Once the fame and fetes have begun to pall, will they remember the peace, the security, and the great common purpose they knew for most of their lives? They may all volunteer for the next expedition.

Extremely Long Journeys

Since the interstellar ships are necessarily self-supporting, there is no theoretical limit to how far they can go. Some writers have suggested that voyages will be undertaken that last many generations. This is possible, I suppose, but does not look very probable. At least, there must be some time beyond which people on Earth will feel it unreasonable to wait. Besides, the longer the period in space, the more chance there is for something to go fatally wrong, with machinery or men. Offhand, I should think that a hundred years in either direction is as much as can be expected of round-trip vessels moving at one-tenth light speed. This barely lets humans reach Epsilon Eridani (116 years off to be exact), though they might stretch a point for an interesting star like Tau Ceti.

But quite likely no "space arks" will ever be built as such. Though the exploratory craft must always be capable of supporting their crews, they may only need to do so while in the other planetary system. The crew members may not experience the decades of voyage at all. Instead, they can lie in suspended animation. Perhaps they will take turns rousing and standing months-long watches, or perhaps the fleet will be entirely under the control of robots. In either case, the travelers will not be aware that an inordinate time has passed.

Suspended animation is a reality for bacteria, whose spores can last many thousands of years. Higher forms of life sometimes exhibit the same ability in a less marked degree. As yet it is only a rather dim possibility for man. Experiments with drugs and with drastic lowering of body temperature point a way that may eventually lead to a technique for "switching off" human life, or for reducing its tempo by a factor of thousands. Unconscious and unaging, the star voyagers will sleep away the years, to awaken when the fleet nears its goal as young as they were.

This would greatly reduce the psychological problems that were mentioned earlier. It should permit more expeditions per century and extend their range. We can well imagine that spacemen and spacewomen, returning to Earth after lifetimes have passed, will find it almost as strange as the planets they explored. Only in their own little corporation will they have any sense of belonging, and after a holiday they will be quite prepared to embark for another new star.

Altogether, then, I think it will be possible to make some extra-Solar voyages within the next few hundred years, even if space technology cannot be radically improved over what is now on our own horizon. But that is a rather big "if." In fact, this whole notion of ships plodding along at eighteen thousand miles a second seems almost as unreal to me as the hyperdrive.

Why should we not be able to travel much faster?

Very High Speeds

When matter moves at a substantial fraction of light velocity, the familiar laws of motion that Newton enunciated are no longer an adequate description of what happens. Mass is not constant but increases with speed; lengths shrink and time contracts. The Einsteinian spaceship—the spaceship traveling at more than half the speed of light—is a different breed from the Newtonian one that we have hitherto considered. Physicists are apt to dismiss it as a fantasy. But if, instead of laughing it off, we examine the problem, we can take heart. The difficulties are admittedly enormous, and we are not going to build any such vessels in the twentieth century. But I see no reason in principle why men should not someday build them if they are willing to pay the considerable price.

For the benefit of the mathematically minded, a technical discussion has been appended to this book. It does not pretend to be exhaustive; indeed, it is nothing but a preliminary sketch. However, it does present some figures. Given a high enough exhaust velocity, it is by no means impossible to travel at speeds on the order of 75 per cent that of light. The Appendix includes remarks on radiation and other dangers and argues that these too can be overcome for the Einsteinian as for the Newtonian ship. This means that Alpha Centauri can be reached in six years, give or take some. Epsilon Eridani is only about fifteen years away.

But these are the transit times according to those who remain behind on Earth. They will be less for the voyagers. When a body travels at high speeds, its time rate, in effect, is reduced. An interval measured "inside" is shorter than one measured "outside." (Actually, the relationship is symmetrical.) This is not mere theory but has been indirectly observed. The decay rates of unstable subatomic particles with extremely great velocities turn out to be less than the decay rates of the same particles at rest with respect to the physicist. As the Appendix shows, an expedition traveling at 75 per cent of light speed covers ten light-years in slightly less than nine years ship time. At 85 per cent of light speed, it takes only a trifle over six years as far as the crew is concerned.

This considerably extends the range of exploration. Suspended animation techniques can extend it still more, so that it becomes very great. But even if this turns out to be impossible, Einsteinian vessels can carry children and grandchildren in the "space ark" style. The time limit of Terrestrial patience, which I set at about one century in the case of the slow(!) interstellar ship, ought to be much lengthened, because the rewards per decade of expedition travel increase with speed. One can imagine the rulers of the future Earth saying, "Another ship just got back with enough information to keep the scientists happy for fifty years. The crew's willing to start out again. Why not?"

The number of stars within a two-hundred-light-year radius is enormous. Even after their planets have been reached, exploration will take centuries. Probably self-supporting bases will be established on those worlds that are most interesting to man because of having gifted natives or strange biochemistries or whatever it may be. These little scientific settlements —men, women, and children—will last for generations, their people traveling about on the surface, mapping, studying, testing, and probing. Much of what they learn can be radioed to Earth. But ships will visit them periodically to pick up the specimens they have gathered, fraternize, bring a few new members, and take home some old ones.

Somewhat less defensible than the Einsteinian ship with a reaction drive is the one with a so-called field drive. This, also discussed in the Appendix, is a vessel that by some unspecified means converts energy directly into speed, without having to eject mass. The mass ratio requirements are less, which means that still higher velocities can be attained—perhaps over 90 per cent that of light. The time contraction is considerably more (for example, a ten-light-year journey at 99 per cent of light speed takes only a year and a half, ship's time) and so the field of exploration is correspondingly enlarged. There are limits here, too. I do not see how even the field drive could crowd light so closely that the galaxy can be circumnavigated in one man's lifetime. It might open, say, a five-hundred- rather than a two-hundred-light-year radius to Earth-centered exploration. But this still leaves us far out in the galactic hinterland.

Of course, occasional crews might not wish to return at all, but may strike off in search of new homes. Chapter 11 will discuss colonization. At present I need only remark that runaways can scarcely affect the rest of mankind. As far as Earth is concerned, they will simply be among those who went out and for some unknown reason were never heard from again.

To sum up the argument, I feel that exploration of our galactic neighborhood is definitely possible and that the transit times will not be unbearably long. True, the explorers will be isolated as men have never been before. If anything goes wrong, there can be no question of rescue. But theirs is a tough breed. Most of them will survive.

The worst perils they will face are more subtle than wild beasts or hostile natives. A few guns or a small atomic bomb should take care of any such menace handily enough—though we hope that our representatives will make every effort to befriend any rational beings they find. I have already claimed that disease will probably not be a great danger; still, the chance cannot be ignored. Though we are not certain today how much biochemical variation there is between the life of one terrestrial planet and another, I suspect that in many cases nothing local can be eaten by men, and a great deal of it may be violently poisonous to them. If so, then careful tests must be made before anyone ventures out in less than a suit of airtight armor, and elaborate precautions must be taken against contaminating the base. Once the terrain and its hazards are fairly well understood, it should often be safe to let the personnel walk about freely. But the odors, the colors, the general weirdness of the countryside will take considerable acclimation.

And, as we have seen, the typical world of interest to us is not likely to resemble Earth even this much. A dim red sun, which occasionally flares toward brilliance and then sinks back; a shadowy, bitterly cold landscape; sometimes a hydrogen atmosphere, liquid ammonia, the dragging of higher gravity than we are used to—all will conspire to remind the explorers that they are strangers in a strange land.

It is not certain how many planets men can ever set foot on. Too strong a gravity could upset the fluid balance of the human organism, with disastrous results. As for subterrestrials, the absence of a magnetic field (due to the absence of a metallic core) may have adverse effects on cell division. No doubt there are other hazards we cannot now predict. We have been shaped by billions of years in one complex environment. Only of late, as we venture into space, have we begun to appreciate how delicately we are in tune with every aspect of this our Earth.

More will be learned in the next few generations. Safe artificial environments can be provided for humans based on planets that are not too big. They can study the giant worlds from natural satellites, sending down telemetric apparatus for a closer look. I do not wish to exaggerate the dangers of interstellar voyaging, only to point out that they exist and that any such expedition will be as complicated and challenging an operation as men have ever undertaken.

Despite the risks and the costs, it will also be among the most rewarding enterprises in history. The spirit of curiosity and adventure drives us. The expansion of our knowledge and power lures us. The prospect of meeting aliens whose ways no man can foresee, from whom we can learn what is now unimaginable, enchants us.

And, finally, there is the hope of colonization.

Chapter 11

New Earth

AS WE OBSERVED EARLIER, a relatively small shift or hesitation in the course of geological events could have postponed the dawn of humanlike consciousness on Earth for several million years. So we can be pretty sure that there are terrestrial planets with life but no natives. Those that are, in addition, habitable to us comprise a minute fraction of the galactic total. Perhaps 1 per cent of the stars in our system have a world that men could settle.

But this is a billion planets.

Before going into whether it is possible or desirable to colonize beyond the Solar System, I should explain the requirement that there be no intelligent natives. First is a crudely practical consideration. Any human settlement will begin small and minimally equipped, living on the verge of disaster. Even after a good foothold is established, expansion into the rest of the land will not be as easy as it was in North America. We need only recall how, here on this friendly Earth, vast regions like central Australia or the Matto Grosso continue to defy exploitation by civilized man. On another planet it would be lunacy to add the opposition of virile indigenous cultures, quick to learn the invaders' military arts, to all the other obstacles.

Such prudence would be irrelevant on a world populated only by feeble savages, who may not even have evolved higher than Pithecanthropus. But I hope that morality will protect them. We have no shadow of a right to their homes. This has not deterred us from seizing the territories of our weaker brethren on Earth. But in all such cases there was some real or imagined economic incentive to do so. There is no money to be made by interstellar colonization, and it cannot remove more than a few thousand people at a time from an overpopulated mother world. We can well afford magnanimity toward other planets.

In fact, the problem is less likely to be one of controlling emigration than of getting any started at all.

Let us consider the questions involved. I have suggested that on interesting worlds there will be scientific bases that may last for generations. But most of them will be confined to structures where an Earth-like environment is artificially maintained. No one will be able to venture outside without elaborate protection. Even where men can walk about unarmored in reasonable safety, the scientists will not occupy everything. Either because there are natives or because the ecology is unsuitable for man, these terrestrial worlds will remain simply objects of study. For that reason, I avoided the word "colony," preferring to reserve it for human settlements that are really intended to be permanent: whose purpose is the ultimate taking over of the planet by man.

Requirements

Clearly, any such world must meet certain physical criteria. It must belong to a star not too unlike Sol, a main-sequence dwarf somewhere between the late F and middle K types. It must have a reasonably stable orbit, though not necessarily perfect. (If calculation shows that orbital changes will make the planet uninhabitable a few million years hence, this scarcely matters to humans.) The path must keep it in the right temperature zone, with enough but not too much ultraviolet as well as visible light. Here we can also be somewhat tolerant. It might be worth while settling a planet so cold that only the tropics are comfortable for man, so hot that only the polar zones and mountaintops are suitable, or otherwise limited. As we shall see, the colonists will adapt over generations, until eventually the badlands are useful to them.

The planet must, of course, be terrestrial so that gravity is not too high for the human fluid balance. Perhaps there is also a lower limit to the weight under which man can spend a lifetime and reproduce. In any event, too small a world will have too thin an atmosphere. I would guess the acceptable range of gravity pull as being from about 0.75 to 1.25 Earth's. If the over-all densities are similar, this implies that colonizable planets have diameters between six thousand and ten thousand miles.

We cannot be sure if the proportion of dry land to water is everywhere the same. Probably it is not. But most terrestrial worlds doubtless have abundant water for human purposes, though not always ideally distributed.

The composition of the crust must be such that there is no serious danger of mineral poisoning, as by large amounts of arsenic in the soil. Perhaps a magnetic field is essential, and no doubt there are other requirements of which we are still unaware. But as I have already tried to prove, these matters seem to depend on a very few parameters such as mass. Therefore we can expect that the average terrestrial globe will resemble Earth geologically—to a close enough approximation.

The atmospheric composition must likewise be rather near our own. Not only oxygen, but carbon dioxide, water vapor, and nitrogen are biologically necessary to us over extended periods of time. Yet too great a concentration is lethal. Here again, though, it looks almost inevitable that life of our basic type will appear and convert the primordial gases into air we can use.

This assumes that it is not loaded with poisons of biological origin. To take a random example, if pollen on Earth causes hay fever in so many people, what might pollens with utterly alien proteins do? Infants exposed to strange materials are especially prone to develop violent allergies. I am afraid that some otherwise promising worlds will be forever off limits to us except for brief visits in sealed armor.

But we need not be too pessimistic about it in general. Parallel evolution must often have taken place. So great is the variety of organic compounds here on Earth that many are bound to be duplicated elsewhere by chance alone—not to mention that similar environments tend to call forth similar biochemical responses. Then, too, immunology is making immense strides. In the future it should be possible to shield everyone against a broad range of allergens and toxins by a few simple treatments given early in life. Or perhaps artificial genetic adjustment can bestow immunities that are thereafter inherited.

It is not enough that the planet be safe to walk on. There must be many such in the galaxy, on which we would nevertheless walk as strangers. For instance, if native proteins are all built of *d*-amino acids, we could get no nourishment from them. Worse, our imported plants and animals could not survive.

We had better not insist that indigenous life forms supply all our needs before we decide to colonize. If so, the chances are very poor of our ever founding any colonies. We should be able to digest a great many exotic *l*-amino proteins—they are broken down and rebuilt in our bodies anyway—and probably the simpler fats, carbohydrates, etc., are duplicated on all planets whose biochemistry is approximately the same as Earth's. But we are unreasonable to demand that every vitamin and other essential compound be present. These we shall have to manufacture or get from our acres planted in Terrestrial vegetables or from specially mutated and bred native species.

If we can do this much, one might ask why we need depend on agriculture at all. Will not food in the future be directly synthesized? In that case, will the colonists ever be farmers at any stage of their history, ever depend on surrounding nature for anything but a few raw materials?

The rebuttal to this argument is threefold. First, though we must certainly not make the mistake of thinking about our settlers in terms of nineteenth-century Dakota sodbusters, the limited cargo capacity of the fleet that brings them may not extend to a dismantled food factory. They may have to plan on a number of years at least, during which they live off the land, before they have the economic surplus to build a chemical industry.

Second, with so many unpredictable hazards, men would be foolish to depend on one or a few manufacturing plants for the necessities of life. This is especially true because such a dependence must slow the expansion of the colony. As we shall see, a rapid initial growth of population is vital. This is much easier if the younger generation has a frontier readily available. Individuals or little groups heading into the wilderness mean a faster enlargement of the economic base than does an attempt to make what is essentially one big "company town" spread outward. I do not mean that the pioneers will, or can, take to the woods with nothing but a gun and an ax, as we romantically imagine the early Americans doing. They will probably depend on the city for a good many necessities, including some of their diet. But the more food and textiles they can produce by themselves, without a large capital investment of elaborate machinery, the better the colony's chances of survival.

The third point is delicate but, I think, the most important. If there cannot be some oneness with nature; if a man cannot raise wheat from Earth or pluck the native fruits clustered overhead; if he cannot strike off afoot for days or weeks at a time, seeking adventure and uncluttered horizons—why should he colonize in the first place? He will only be trading one over-mechanized existence for another. And he will lose by the exchange, for a completely isolated small town, which no one ever dares leave, must grow incredibly dull. Bear in mind that we are not talking now about a scientific base, whose purpose is simply the accumulation of knowledge. We are dealing with people who want a home, for their descendants as well as themselves.

Altogether, then, I think an ecology into which man can fit is a basic requirement for colonization. The fit need not be perfect, but there should be a prospect, not too remote, of eventually approaching perfection. If our grains grow poorly, we should be able to create new strains that thrive. If it is not practical to keep dogs, we should be able to tame some local species. If we cannot live indefinitely off wild plants and animals, we should be able to do so temporarily, and in the course of time our descendants should be better able to do so. For we plan to remain here as long as this world endures.

Planting the Colony

Granted such a planet, the barriers to our possession of it are still tremendous. First there is distance. Perhaps Tau Ceti,

Epsilon Eridani, or some other local star has a suitable attendant. Though these suns are cooler than Sol, a terrestrial globe may have a close orbit. But the odds are against it. We shall in all probability have to extend our search fifty or more light-years. If Einsteinian spaceships were built today, it would still be a matter of centuries before colonization could begin. The subject of this chapter is remote from our immediate concerns. But then, so is the whole book. Yet the wish to think beyond our own lifetimes is part of our nature, a part that may in the end redeem us from the blind greed and bloodlust that are also born in us.

The cargo that can be carried by any readily designable high-velocity spaceship is sharply limited in both bulk and mass. And it is not likely that a large number of such vessels will ever be in existence at any one time. So the colonizing fleet can take no more than some hundreds of people—a few thousands at most—with minimal equipment for their use. No doubt the thousands are only possible if they can be put in suspended animation. One shudders at what would happen otherwise, if they were crammed wakeful together for decade after decade.

Having arrived, the settlers will establish themselves at a location selected by the explorers who preceded them and who spent years on the planet, learning everything they could, before returning home to certify that it was habitable. The fleet will remain in orbit while the regular crews collect reaction mass for the return journey and help the colonists do the essential construction work. But after some time, probably less than a year, the ships will start back.

And then the great loneliness will set in.

There should be radio contact with Earth. But that is a ghostly thread of talk, years or generations old, ever less meaningful to the settlers. Once in a great while, perhaps, a fleet will arrive with new immigrants—each arrival an important historic event, and each successive load of people more foreign to the pioneer stock. Certainly no help will ever come from outside when trouble arises. For all practical purposes, these folk have been cut adrift to live or die as best they can.

Many will die. Accidents, bad weather, overwork, undernourishment, deadly circumstances that the explorers failed to observe, will take a heavy toll of the first generations. The strangenesses we have discussed, the manifold problems of establishing an ecological niche as well as an industrial base for themselves, cannot easily or cheaply be mastered. Whole colonies may perish miserably, as the Greenland settlement of the Norsemen did. Others will fight their way toward a better life, and achieve it, but at an appalling human cost—as the New Englanders did.

There will be a driving need for population growth. Plainly the group must make up losses, provide more hands for work, and widen its margin of safety. Women must bear as many children as they are able, and bury not a few. Old age will be honored simply because it is proof of exceptional hardihood and foresight.

The most important reason for breeding as fast as possible is less direct than those above. Since the colony is small, it has a correspondingly limited reservoir of individual heredity. Out of this gene pool, as it is called, must come the heredity of the entire human stock for this planet, barring what few immigrants arrive later. Now, every man or woman has the potential of bringing forth a rather wide variety of children, taller or shorter, lighter or darker, and so on through every trait, including some hidden but extremely important matters of individual biochemistry. If a parent has only a few offspring, most of this potential is lost. Geneticists have often observed that when a species is rare in some area, sheer chance can cause the disappearance of many inherited features. The individuals that might have transmitted them never happen to be born, or die by accident before they reproduce.

This process, genetic drift, could destroy some valuable characteristics in the colony. Total species degeneration is not impossible. Moreover, biological adaptation to a new environment requires variants for natural selection to work upon. For example, an ability to withstand cold or to get along on an unusually low ration of vitamin D would be useful on the chill planet of a reddish star. People with that kind of metabolism would have an easier life than others; on the whole, they would produce more than their share of offspring; slowly, over the centuries, men would become better fitted to this world.

But such hereditary variation is of no racial use if it is never passed on.

Reproduction will therefore be imperative in the early period of an extra-Solar colony. Teen-age marriages will be the norm. Mothers of large broods will gain social status. Coupling this with the desirability of independent pioneering outside the original settlement, we can see how a patriarchal, family-centered culture might well develop. However, to promote variability, these families must be strictly exogamous. Marriages between cousins will probably be forbidden.

Yet equally possible is a highly permissive attitude toward sexual relations: not unlike that of the Eskimos, who also colonized under difficult conditions. Illegitimacy may confer no stigma on parents or children, and even married women may be encouraged to have offspring by several different men. The social unit may become the large clan rather than the small family.

Despite every effort to expand the gene pool, it may remain dangerously small. Artificial insemination, using sperm from Earth, may help. A more speculative but theoretically possible way to get around the problem is by exogenesis. Both sperm and ova from donors who remained at home could be carried along with the fleet, kept alive until needed by suspended animation techniques or something corresponding. When the colony is well established, these cells could then be artificially united and fetuses grown to term in the laboratory. Each family could be required by law to adopt one or more such babies. In that case the fleet can carry a million potential new individuals along, and the danger of genetic drift is eliminated. Incidentally, livestock could also be transported by such means, and may be even if it is not considered desirable to do so for humans.

Another, still hazier possibility is genetic manipulation. But though I feel confident that some control of heredity will be feasible in times to come, the addition of whole new biological characteristics may prove too tricky. I also rather dislike the idea on philosophical grounds. Of course, my descendants may regard the matter otherwise.

Slowly, then, with toil and sacrifice and luck, the colonists will build a real home for themselves. In time they will occupy the entire planet. Evolution will modify them in many subtle ways, until at last they would no longer feel comfortable on Earth. More striking will be the evolution of their society. Cut off almost entirely from the rest of the human race, faced with enormous and unprecedented problems, malleable to individuals with new ideas, the civilization will develop into something unique. Surely each world that is colonized will bring forth at least one fresh breed of man and at least one culture such as exists nowhere else.

Rewards

But why should an ambitious project like this be undertaken at all? No matter how rich the Terrestrial community of the future is—and I suspect that it will be poor, with great wealth reserved for the very few—the cost of exploring and planting a colony beyond the Solar System must be immense. Any thought of commerce or imperialism at the Einsteinian snail's pace is ludicrous. Were the other planet an Eden to which men simply needed transportation, its settlement might paradoxically be impossible. Outraged taxpayers could rebel at the thought of meeting an exorbitant price to benefit a mere handful. It is just as well that the prospect before the settlers will be one the average Earthling does not envy. We can even imagine that Machiavellian propaganda will exaggerate the dangers and hardships.

Conceivably a private group that wished to leave Earth could raise the funds themselves. They might be well-to-do political, religious, or social dissenters, unhappy at the course of events. Or the government itself might want to get rid of such misfits as gently as possible. Bound by laws protecting minorities, or simply unwilling to stir up a hornet's nest, the leaders of Earth could offer passage to a whole new world where the nonconformists might live as they chose. Massachusetts, Pennsylvania, and Maryland had this origin. Georgia and Botany Bay are less pleasant cases, which may perhaps have analogues in the future. Besides disposing of trouble-makers, officialdom would get kudos for a bold new work.

We can imagine a few other immediately practical motives for starting extra-Solar colonies. But history moves on, and nothing is as dead as yesterday's hardheaded realism. The true benefits of spreading out into the galaxy are long-range, immensely transcending any hopes that confine themselves to this one little planet. If they are only slightly more farsighted and altruistic than we are, our descendants will need no material inducement. The sense of high purpose, the surety that distant generations will honor them for what they began, may in the end prove enough to carry them starward.

Even today, when fewer than a dozen men have pierced our sky, we can see what some of the real rewards must be. First, colonization means potential immortality for the human genus. Man's safety on Earth was never great, and it dwindles hourly. Disarmament, even world government, will not guarantee survival in an age when population presses natural resources to the limit and when the knowledge of how to work mischief on a planetary scale is ever more widely diffused among peoples who may grow ever more desperate. True, the present crisis must somehow be surmounted; a measure of stability must one way or another be achieved. If not, machine civilization is finished and humans never will have stargoing ships. But granted that we erect a world order of sorts, we dare not assume that it will endure forever. The stablest empires of the past cracked open in the end.

If racial suicide appears unlikely to you, let the scarred Moon remind you that there have been cosmic disasters in the past. Given sufficient time, they will happen again. Even now a dark star or rogue planet may be on a collision course with Earth. Conceded, the probability is very small. But the magnitude of the event is such that a few colonial ventures are exceedingly cheap insurance. And eventually the Sun is sure to consume its own children. If there are men on other spheres, whatever may happen at home, the race will live.

Closer at hand lies the prospect of knowledge. Some communication will surely be maintained with the settlers, however rare and slow it may be. Explorers cannot discover everything about a world; they are not there long enough. Scientists based on planets uninhabitable by man are confined in their activities. But colonists, each generation more intimate with their new home, can tell the savants of Earth about it in nearly infinite detail. A report on a new species of extra-Terrestrial bacteria may not sound spectacular, but it will confer a deeper understanding of life as a many-faceted universal phenomenon than will any amount of superficial naked-eye description.

Sociologists, psychologists, and historians will be fascinated by the millennial unfolding of colonial civilizations. A brighter light will be thrown on man himself, his depths and potentialities, the laws by which he and his societies evolve. With the help of such knowledge, maybe the too small sum of human happiness can be increased a little; more important, the human spirit may grow a little. The example of the colonists is apt to be the more stimulating because they will be a virile and adventurous breed. No one who was not can have survived to become any important part of their ancestry.

In time, however, they too will reach the physical limits of their worlds, they too will be settling down in unity. The threat of stagnation will arise for them as it did long ago for Earth. Then all human beings everywhere should welcome any outside stimulus. Communication between diverse colonial civilizations and the mother planet may even prove more valuable over the centuries than communication with nonhuman races whose problems and dreams are, after all, nonhuman. Just so has the example of America profoundly affected European history, and vice versa.

But the act of colonization will in itself extend man's radius of action. Once a planet's economic problems begin to come under control, its citizens are fairly sure to start their own quest for alien intelligences, listening with radio telescopes and calling with radio beams. And they will build spaceships, sending out explorers and settlers of their own.

This can be done rather early in the development of a successful colony. Instead of plundering the planet heedlessly, the new civilizations—we hope—will heed the lesson of the past and make sensible use of their resources. They will be the more prone to do so because their approach to industry and agriculture had to be highly scientific from the beginning if they were to survive at all. In any event, they need not waste raw materials in the course of learning, as we today, for instance, are wasting petroleum on piston engines because we have not mastered the details of obviously better designs like the turbine. The first generation of colonists will have brought microfilmed libraries telling them how to do such things right.

So we can expect that a few centuries after its founding the typical daughter society will still have a moderate population density and abundant natural resources together with a large and sophisticated industrial plant. This means great wealth per capita. A space fleet should be easier for such a world to maintain than for Earth. Memories of their own glorified past will spur the people on to undertake space travel. With uncommon exceptions, they will be free of the economic and political difficulties that made the initial Earth-centered effort so great.

Thus man will spread among the stars—and not so dreadfully slowly. The number of colonies will tend to grow geometrically. Over a long period of time, the front of the human wave will advance at some average rate, which it seems conservative to put at a light-year per century.

No doubt other races are carrying on the same endeavor. They need not be a large proportion of all the intelligent species to be a vast absolute number. And if, as I should certainly imagine, the development of a civilization able to colonize in space is one of the irreversible revolutions in anyone's history, then the number will grow with time. More and more, men will meet their peers face to face.

This will not cause any great rivalry. Most of the others are seeking worlds useless to man. The cases where two sets of explorers claim the same planet must be vanishingly rare. If it ever does occur, it may or may not lead to a minor clash on the scene, but there can be no question of war fought over interstellar distances. Joint colonization is not unthinkable, and could lead to some extraordinarily interesting societies. On the whole, these encounters of man and androde cannot but be of immense mutual value.

So we will go on, century after outward-looking century, discovering who knows what, growing in knowledge and wisdom as we travel. At a light-year per century, it would take us three million years to reach the heart of the galaxy. But our explorers will always outrun our colonists. The sphere of their activity can expand at almost half the top speed of their ships—allowing for the fact that they must return home. The sphere of knowledge can grow still faster if radio waves are used to communicate. Left to ourselves, we might perhaps hear first-accounts of the blazing galactic nucleus in less than a hundred thousand years.

But we are not going to be left to ourselves. The older and higher races, some of them at least, must be moving outward. One day their emissaries will meet ours. I think that by then stargoing man will have enough greatness of his own to learn what the elders have to teach, and carry it back homeward. Our finest flowering may date from that moment. And we need not be passive disciples. The universe has something to learn from us, too.

But although that age of enlightenment may not be far off as they reckon time in the cosmos, it is admittedly distant in terms of a mortal man's life. Few people will ever go spaceward with more than the vaguest thought of an ultimate destiny. They will go because they are curious, prideful, desirous of freedom, eager to improve the lot of the next generation.

And I feel that those are the really important reasons for seeking out the stars. Let the remote tomorrows come as they will. For us—even those of us who stay behind and wistfully hearken to travelers' tales—our enterprise beyond the sky will keep alive that sense of bravery, wonder, and achievement without which man would hardly be himself.

Appendix

The Einsteinian Spaceship

WHEN A BODY moves at a substantial fraction of light velocity, the Newtonian laws of mechanics are no longer a good enough approximation and the Einsteinian relativistic forms must be used instead. If spaceships are to reach the stars in anything like reasonable time, they shall have to have such speeds—unless they evade the whole problem by a "hyperdrive." At present it is idle to speculate about devices like that, which in all probability never will be invented. But one can make a few meaningful preliminary remarks about travel at Einsteinian velocities.

Without postulating a radical new physics, I can only imagine three ways to propel a spaceship. One is by the pressure of light, but plainly this would not work at great distances from the Sun. The second is by a reaction drive. Mass is expelled, producing a thrust in the opposite direction. The third is more speculative, a "field drive" that in some way accelerates the ship without having to shoot out mass. Let us consider the last two in that order.

Reaction Drive

The basic equation for reactive acceleration of a mass m to a velocity v is

$$m\,dv = -\,k\,dm, \tag{1}$$

where k is the velocity of expelled mass, the exhaust velocity. (I use k rather than the c of the rocket engineer because in physics c stands for the velocity of light in free space, a quantity with which we shall have considerable dealings.)

Integrating Equation 1, we obtain

$$r = \frac{m_1}{m_2} = e^{v/k}, \tag{2}$$

where m_1 is the initial mass (ship plus payload plus fuel) before acceleration, when the velocity is taken to be zero, and m_2 is the mass remaining (ship plus payload plus any unexpended fuel) at velocity v. The number e, of course, is the base of natural logarithms, approximately 2.72. The quantity r is known as the mass ratio.

Let us assume throughout that the ship moves in free space. As observed in Chapter 10, it will not be landing on any planets. The ship must escape the gravitational control of its home star and perform various maneuvers, but this turns out to require such a low proportion of the total reaction mass that it can be included under "payload." We will also assume that the stars are at rest with respect to each other. This is not unrealistic, since their relative motions are small compared to the speed of light.

The ship must decelerate as it approaches the goal. Under our assumptions, Equation 2 is applicable again. But the total mass ratio, first to accelerate and then to decelerate, is not simply twice that needed to reach v, but the square of it. For example, if r to reach a certain speed is 3, the ship must start out with nine times its terminal mass if it is to brake itself. Let us call the total acceleration-plus-deceleration mass ratio R, so that

$$R = r^2. \qquad (3)$$

Thus far we have treated the Newtonian case, in which the ship reaches a speed that is only a tiny fraction of that of light. We wish now to find r and R for the Einsteinian case. The laws of relativity that will concern us are the following:

If the mass of a body at rest with respect to the observer is m_0, then the mass m that the observer will measure as the body moves with a uniform velocity v with respect to him is

$$m = m_0\left(1 - \frac{v^2}{c^2}\right)^{-1/2}, \qquad (4)$$

where c, to repeat, is the velocity of light *in vacuo*.

This is the basic reason for the light-speed limitation. As v

approaches closer and closer to c, m becomes greater and greater. At light speed m would become infinite. But this is physically as well as logically impossible, since it becomes progressively harder to accelerate so massive a body. Not that anyone aboard the ship would find it, or himself, heavier. He would observe himself as traveling through a universe where the mass of everything else had increased according to Equation 4 and where a length l_0, as measured at rest, was now shrunk to

$$l = l_0 \left(1 - \frac{v^2}{c^2}\right)^{1/2}. \qquad (5)$$

An interval of time that one observer (either at home or aboard the ship) experienced as T_0, would be measured by the other as

$$T = T_0 \left(1 - \frac{v^2}{c^2}\right)^{1/2}. \qquad (6)$$

This is the famous "time paradox" of relativity. A fast-moving observer lives at a much slower rate than one that is at rest. In the case of a uniform velocity, the relationship is symmetrical: each observer measures the other's time rate as having been slowed. But a spaceship must accelerate and decelerate, not merely with respect to Earth, but with respect to the entire universe, that is, the general background of the stars. This introduces an asymmetry, which takes the question out of special and into general relativity. It turns out that a spaceman who made a round trip at some high speed v would return younger than the girl he left behind him in the proportion indicated by Equation 6—neglecting the periods during which he was under positive or negative acceleration.

The kinetic energy of the spaceship is simply the energy equivalent of the added mass, and vice versa. That is, since the total energy equals mc^2, the kinetic energy is

$$\text{K.E.} = m_0c^2 \left[\frac{1}{\left(1 - \frac{v^2}{c^2}\right)^{1/2}} - 1\right]. \qquad (7)$$

Let us for convenience introduce one more quantity,

$$B = \frac{v}{c}, \tag{8}$$

the fraction of light speed at which the ship moves when it has attained maximum velocity. It is always less than unity. We can now ask ourselves what the requirements are for reaching any given B.

The equation giving r for the relativistic case has been worked out at various times by different men.[1] I am indebted to Oliver Saari for doing it on my behalf. Being a much better mathematician than I, he must not be held responsible for any errors in my presentation or use of his results.

The derivation is too long for me to present more than a summary here, though that should be enough to allow anyone with some education in these matters to reconstruct the whole. One begins with a differential equation relating the increase in velocity, dv, to the decrease in mass, $-dm$, as measured from the ship. It has the same form as Equation 1, which is hardly surprising; the ship is always motionless with respect to itself. Then the quantities involved are transformed into those that an unaccelerated observer, taken to be at rest, for example, on Earth, would measure. Velocities are compounded according to relativistic rules, and a differential equation is obtained, which can be expanded by the binomial theorem. Taking limiting values, one derives a new differential equation relating mass and velocity as measured by an observer at rest. On integration, we get the algebraic equation we wish, the relativistic

$$r = \left(\frac{1+B}{1-B}\right)^{c/2k}. \tag{9}$$

As is to be expected, it reduces to Equation 2 for small values of B.

Squaring both sides of Equation 9 gives us

$$R = \left(\frac{1+B}{1-B}\right)^{c/k}, \tag{10}$$

which represents the mass ratio needed to accelerate to a

velocity v, "coast" there until the destination is approached, and then decelerate. This will be a one-way trip unless R itself is squared—but that makes a ridiculously huge mass ratio—or reaction mass can be obtained at the destination. The latter is a plausible scheme, as explained in Chapter 10.

The values of a few typical R's are summarized in the following table for several values of B and k/c.

Table 2

k/c	B = 0.25	0.50	0.75	0.85	0.90	0.99
0.25	7.6	81.0	2,401	23,001	130,321	1.6×10^9
0.50	2.75	9	49	151	361	39,601
0.75	1.97	4.3	13.4	28.4	50.6	1,162
1	1.67	3.0	7.0	12.3	19	199

A few things are immediately obvious. With a k substantially less than one-half c, there is no chance of going even half as fast as light. Even in the limiting case where k is equal to c itself, the maximum speed seems to be under nine-tenths that of light. However, given high exhaust velocities, lower than many already attained in particle accelerators, it is not absurd to think about traveling somewhere between one-half and, say, five-sixths light speed.

Clearly this cannot be done with chemical fuels. The fission-powered ion drive may eventually be improved until it can deliver exhaust velocities like those we are considering. But I think a more hopeful prospect is hydrogen fusion. Admittedly all attempts so far to control this reaction in the laboratory have failed. But despite the publicity they got, they were not made with the massive seriousness that could have been applied, and someday will be. That last phrase is a safe prediction. An industrial society cannot continue forever burning coal, oil, and uranium. These reserves are finite. Sooner or later, and probably sooner rather than later, fusion reactions must be carried out for constructive as well as destructive purposes. If this is impossible, then in the long run the survival of machine civilization is impossible and all talk about interstellar travel is empty. But since no natural law appears to forbid the project's succeeding, I think that in time it will, if only our culture holds together.

A fusion motor could presumably expel nuclei (and electrons, to preserve a charge balance) at extremely high velocities. It might do this directly, for example, spitting out helium ions under the control of a magnetic field as they are formed. Another possibility might be an adaptation of the linac system. The ultimate reaction engine would convert matter to energy with 100 per cent efficiency, realizing the full 9×10^{20} ergs that are in each gram (minus the toll exacted by the laws of thermodynamics), and emit mass in the form of radiation. This is represented by the last line of Table 2. A less awesome device is assumed in the line above it, where matter is expelled at three-fourths *c*. Even in that case, speeds on the order of three-fourths that of light look possible for the ship.

Some readers may object that acceleration times will be too long. At one gravity acceleration (980 cm/sec^2) it takes 355 days to reach the speed of light, or 267 days to reach three-fourths *c*—a not inconsiderable part of the whole voyage. (The time contraction effect reduces this for the crew, but not by very much.) And it assumes what may be an unrealistically powerful thrust. Would not a ship which started out with a mass ratio of, say, 20, be unable to expel matter fast enough to accelerate at a decent rate? Might it not take years to reach its maximum speed?

The answer can be given if we divide Equation 1 by dt, remembering that the ship is always a Newtonian system with respect to itself. If k is three-fourths c and the mass of ship plus payload is ten thousand metric tons, the ship can have an initial acceleration of one gravity by expelling 0.43 R kilograms per second, or 8.6 Kg/sec for $R=20$. (The gravitational field of the Sun reduces this acceleration only negligibly.)

This much mass per se should be easy to handle. It is the rate at which work must be done—at which the motors must develop energy—that may prove troublesome. Under the assumptions of the previous paragraph it amounts to about 3.9×10^{24} ergs/sec (relativistic calculation) or 3.9×10^{5} mega-megawatts. This is equivalent to the conversion of matter into energy at the rate of some four Kg/sec. Though the requirement drops steadily as ship mass decreases, this does not happen very fast, and an output on this order of magnitude must be kept up for a long time. Whatever nuclear process is the source of power, even if 99 per cent of the energy is released as exhaust velocity, there will still be a great amount of gamma radiation, from which the crew must somehow be protected. Perhaps a dumbbell-shaped spaceship is the best design, with living quarters and propulsion mechanism widely separated. Then only a small part of the motor section need be heavily shielded: that part from which the radiation can reach the living quarters.

To be sure, acceleration is most difficult at the very start, when the system has its greatest mass. At the end of the voyage, when deceleration is over and the ship is maneuvering on the small amount of reaction mass included under "payload," a given acceleration can be maintained by employing only $1/R$ the thrust of the initial stage. So the voyagers may well depart at a low acceleration, which gradually increases as the months go by. The deceleration toward journey's end would increase likewise, beginning with the terminal value of acceleration and ending at one gravity or whatever the desired maximum is. All in all, I conclude that the acceleration problem is soluble, though it may add months to the total voyage time.

That voyage will take years at best, and readers may feel that ten thousand tons is too little to support a number of persons for so long—besides the vessel itself and whatever equipment will be needed at the destination. As yet we know so little about the requirements that we cannot be dogmatic. But I suspect that not only the main craft but the propulsion devices, the exploratory boats, and most other apparatus can be built extremely light—by the time space technology has gotten to the point of interstellar ventures. For instance, given a k on the order of three-fourths c, the R needed for interplanetary velocity changes of about a hundred kilometers per second is almost ridiculously small. Moreover, a boat could make an aerodynamic landing on any planet with an atmosphere. If he wishes, the reader may multiply my ten thousand tons by a factor of several without affecting the argument too much, especially since an interstellar expedition is more likely to be made by a fleet than by a single ship, so that no one vessel need carry everything that will be needed.

As for the humans aboard, a few tons per person should

take care of their biological requirements. The ship will have to include an ecologically closed system in any event, where all wastes are recycled to produce new food, air, water, etc. Systems of this type have long been discussed in the literature, for example, hydroponics under sun lamps to furnish vegetables and regenerate oxygen. Even allowing for physiological needs such as engineers today often overlook (for instance, magnetic flux), it is hard to imagine how a very large proportion of the total mass can be needed to keep the personnel alive. Their mental health is another matter, discussed in Chapter 10. It can also be well provided for.

Even so, it is desirable to shorten the voyage as much as possible. Table 3, below, gives paired values of the time needed to cross ten light-years at certain values of B. The time T_0 is measured outside the ship by an observer at rest, for example, on Earth. The time T is that measured inside the ship according to Equation 6.

Table 3

B	T_0 (years)	T (years)
0.5	20.0	17.4
0.75	13.3	8.95
0.85	11.6	6.05

The advantages of traveling at high speeds thus turn out to be even greater than would appear at first glance. For relatively short voyages, say, two or three light-years, the gain from using a very large R would scarcely be counterbalanced by any shortening of T, especially since acceleration time would be increased. But the longer the hop, the more worth while a larger R, with its correspondingly high B, becomes; and the smaller is the proportion of total mass added by each person aboard. Thus we can expect that ships intended for long interstellar voyages will be as large as feasible and have quite good-sized crews. Their T may in some cases be little greater than the T of craft making considerably shorter trips.

A formidable obstacle is interstellar hydrogen. This occurs in a concentration of one atom per cubic centimeter, approximately, so that a ship traveling at velocity v cm/sec will strike that many atoms per square centimeter of cross-sectional area.

At speeds comparable to light's, this is equivalent to a horrifying blast of radiation: something like fifty million roentgens per hour at three-fourths *c*, with less than a thousand roentgens being lethal. Material shielding will be of scant value, especially as outright erosion wears it away.

But though the problem is difficult, it is not insoluble, at least in principle. Ships traveling within the Solar System, especially to Venus and Mercury, will provide a demand and a testing ground for radiation screens. Solar flares alone suggest that much! The continued development of magnetohydrodynamics, still an infant science, should result in nonmaterial means of deflecting energetic particles. This is the more likely when we consider that a fusion engine itself implies a high level of magnetohydrodynamic technology. Fields adequate to control particles emitted at three-fourths *c* for propulsion, should be adequate to deflect particles with which one collides at a similar speed.

In fact, the motor itself could perhaps be the screen generator. Have the propulsive mechanism in the forward section of the dumbbell-shaped vessel, rather than aft. The reaction mass will stream past the crew's shell without touching it. Let the motor be exposed to space, so that there is no metal shield to be worn away. The hydrogen atoms that the ship encounters would probably be ionized by the sheer violence of the collision with the screen field; or if not, an ionizing device can be provided. (Or there might even be an adroit use of whatever leverage is offered by an atom's electromagnetic asymmetries.) Given all this, the control fields of the fusion motor should deflect the interstellar wind. Of course, this system cannot be used if it turns out that the reaction mass blast irradiates the crew section too much.

Alternatively, the gas of space might be scooped up and used as fuel and ram jet reaction mass. A broad enough scoop field would enable the ship to "live off the country," meeting all its energy and mass requirements, once the speed was sufficiently great. This would permit continuous acceleration and the attainment of velocities very close indeed to *c*.[2] But I am not sure that it is really feasible. I do suggest, however, that enough energy can be acquired by fusion of the hydrogen that is encountered to operate the radiation screen itself once acceleration has ceased and to meet the crew's energy needs.

Meteoritic particles may or may not prove to be a hazard. The chance of encountering a large boulder between the stars looks vanishingly small. But any bit of gravel could destroy a ship at three-fourths *c*. Perhaps the fusion reaction in the motor, if it is carried forward, can vaporize whatever penetrates the electromagnetic screens; or a laser beam might gasify any object detected by an ultrasensitive analogue of radar.

Interstellar navigation will be difficult. Not only will the Doppler effect discolor the stars and aberration displace them in the apparent sky, but the precise location of the target star may not be known exactly. Though we can expect astronomical measurements to become greatly refined in the future, a small percentage of error adds up to a lot of absolute distance when light-years are involved. Having ended deceleration, the voyagers could be forced to plod for years at mere interplanetary velocities before actually reaching their goal. This possibly disastrous annoyance can be avoided, or reduced to manageable dimensions, by first sending unmanned vessels to get accurate data. These, being quite small, can have very high *R*'s, which will not only shorten transit time but allow considerable maneuvering at the end. Automatically unfolding outsize radio transmitters, they can send their data several light-years back to base.

There are many other dangers and problems that we can imagine, and no doubt unsuspected ones will appear in the future. Interstellar travel is so vast an undertaking that it dwarfs our interplanetary efforts nearly to insignificance. And yet the interplanetary work, scarcely begun, has already met and overcome difficulties that are several orders of magnitude greater than any encountered in the development of aeronautics since Kitty Hawk. Knowledge and skill grow almost exponentially. So does the wealth of society as a whole, in absolute though probably not in per capita terms—provided that war, population density, and waste of natural resources do not get completely out of hand. Is it unbelievable that the world a hundred years or five hundred or a thousand years hence can spend thousands of times as much on interstellar exploration as it is now spending on the race to the Moon?

The proportion of its total economy thus used may be no greater than the proportion of our economy that we devote to astronautics at this moment.

The conclusion I draw from the present inquiry is that travel to the stars, at velocities on the order of 75 per cent light speed, is possible and can be made feasible. An enormous research and development effort is required, probably taking at least a century from its inception to the first manned extra-Solar voyage. But the goal can be attained if mankind wants it enough.

Field Drive

Thus far we have considered ships using reaction engines, that is, expelling mass to get a propulsive force. Some theorists have played with the idea of a vessel that accelerates by use of a different principle. A running man does not eject mass to get up speed. Is there some way by which a spaceship could enjoy the same advantage?

Conceivably it might exert a push against galactic magnetic fields, thereby generating an opposite force on itself. This looks quantitatively most insufficient but suggests vaguely what could perhaps be done. If gravity control is possible, we can imagine a spaceship that is propelled by a negative force —reacting, in a way, against all the stars aft of it. Getting still farther from orthodox science, we might wonder if the accepted laws of motion tell the whole story. William O. Davis and others have suggested that transient phenomena necessarily violate, or at least supplement, Newton's third law and may therefore provide an opening wedge for engineers.

I am not here concerned with whether any such notion is true, only with its significance. Let us assume that an engine has been built that can accelerate a spaceship without expelling mass. I will call this a "field drive" for lack of a better term. The name implies that propulsion is furnished by some kind of force field, but we need not worry today whether the implication makes sense.

In effect, a field drive—provided it obeys the law of conservation of mass-energy—converts some of the mass it carries directly into velocity. This seems like a more efficient process than the reaction drive, where mass must be thrown overboard. Let us investigate how much more.

The kinetic energy of a ship that has attained a velocity v is given by Equation 7. In this case, m_0 is the same as the m_2 of Equation 2, though of course the mass ratio now is not equal to the quantity there given. Instead, if m_e is the mass converted to energy,

$$r_f = \frac{m_2 + m_e}{m_2} = \frac{m_2 + m_2\left[\frac{1}{(1 - B^2)^{1/2}} - 1\right]}{m_2}$$
$$= (1 - B^2)^{-1/2} \qquad (11)$$

and

$$R_f = r_f^2 = \frac{1}{1 - B^2}. \qquad (12)$$

The subscript f is used to indicate that these are the mass ratios required by the field drive, as opposed to those required by the reaction drive. The following table lists values of R_f for various B.

Table 4

B =	0.25	0.50	0.75	0.85	0.90	0.99
R_f =	1.06	1.33	2.38	3.56	5.25	50.0

It is far more encouraging than Table 2. If R_f is as great as 20, speeds of almost 0.97 c can be reached. This means a time factor of 0.22, so that T for a ten-light-year crossing amounts to only a little over two years. To be sure, at such speeds the hazards already mentioned are proportionately greater, but we may assume that they can be overcome.

There are limits to the advantages. On the highly implausible assumption that a B of 0.99 can be reached, the time factor dwindles to 0.14 and a fifty-light-year crossing can be made in a T of seven years. This is not negligible to the crew; but fifty light-years is nearly negligible to the galaxy. In short, though the field drive would make interstellar travel faster and easier than the reaction drive, man's exploration of the universe would not be tremendously hastened. And it has yet to be shown that a field drive is possible at all.

Chapter References

PUBLICATION DATA for nonfiction books are in the Bibliography. "AAAS" indicates citation of a lecture delivered at the 1961 meeting in Denver of the American Association for the Advancement of Science, on the date specified.

Chapter 1

1. Halton Arp, "Stellar Content of Galaxies," *Science*, 134, (Sept. 22, 1961), p. 818.
2. Maurice M. Shapiro, "Supernovae as Cosmic-Ray Sources," *Science*, 135 (Jan. 19, 1962).
3. Halton Arp, "Evolution of Stars and Galaxies," AAAS, Dec. 28.
4. Shapiro, *op. cit.*, p. 181.
5. Arp, "Evolution of Stars and Galaxies."
6. G. R. Burbidge, "The Origin of the Chemical Elements," AAAS, Dec. 28.
7. Cecilia Payne-Gaposchkin, *Stars in the Making*, p. 20.
8. *Ibid.*, p. 150.
9. Arp, "Stellar Content of Galaxies," pp. 810–13.
10. Payne-Gaposchkin, *op. cit.*, pp. 119–31.
11. Fred Hoyle, *Frontiers of Astronomy*, pp. 274–81.
12. Arp, "Evolution of Stars and Galaxies."
13. Arp, "Stellar Content of Galaxies," pp. 818–19.
14. Peter van de Kamp, "The Nearest Stars," *American Scientist*, 42, 4 (Oct. 1954).
15. Payne-Gaposchkin, *op. cit.*, pp. 147–48.
16. Hoyle, *op cit.*, pp. 83–90.
17. Harold C. Urey, *The Planets: Their Origin and Development*, pp. 122–23.
18. Hoyle, *op. cit.*, p. 95.
19. William A. Fowler, "Nuclear Clues to the Early History of the Solar System," *Science*, 135 (March 23, 1962).
20. Su-Shu Huang, "Life Outside the Solar System," *Scientific American*, 202, 4 (April 1960), p. 61 (citing Otto Struve).
21. *Ibid.*, pp. 58–60.
22. Van de Kamp, *op. cit.*, p. 586.

Chapter 2

1. Carl Sagan, "Interstellar Panspermia," AAAS, Dec. 27.
2. *Ibid.*
3. J. D. Bernal, "The Problem of Stages in Biopoesis," in Oparin *et al.* (eds.), *Proceedings of the First International Symposium on the Origin of Life on the Earth*, p. 39.
4. Cited in Harold C. Urey, *The Planets: Their Origin and Development*, p. 150.
5. Sidney W. Fox, "How Did Life Begin?" *Science*, 132 (July 22, 1960), p. 200.
6. *Ibid.*, p. 201.
7. Carl Sagan, "On the Origin and Planetary Distribution of Life," *Radiation Research*, 15, 2 (August 1961), p. 177.
8. *Ibid.*, pp. 175–76.
9. *Ibid.*
10. Philip H. Abelson, "The Role of the Primitive Environment in Shaping the Course of the Origin of Life," AAAS, Dec. 28.
11. J. D. Bernal, *The Physical Basis of Life*, pp. 34–35.
12. A. I. Oparin, *The Origin of Life on the Earth*, pp. 301–41.
13. Fox, *op. cit.*, pp. 201–05.
14. *Idem.*, "The Borders of Biochemical Evolution," AAAS, Dec. 27.
15. *Ibid.*
16. Oparin, *op. cit.*, pp. 347–93.
17. Bernal, *The Physical Basis of Life*, p. 47.
18. I. E. El'piner and A. V. Sokol'skaya, "The Part Played by Acoustic Energy in the Initiation of Chemical Processes Under Natural Conditions," in Oparin *et al.* (eds.), *Proceedings of the First International Symposium on the Origin of Life on the Earth*, pp. 172–73.

Chapter 3

1. F. D. Sisler in E. M. Fallone (ed.), *Proceedings of Lunar and Planetary Exploration Colloquium*, pp. 67–73.
2. Carl Sagan, "Organic Matter and Life in Meteorites," *op. cit.*, p. 49.
3. W. G. Meinschein *et al., op. cit.*, pp. 54–67.
4. Philip H. Abelson, "Factors Limiting the Long Term Viability of Organisms," AAAS, Dec. 27.
5. Harold C. Urey, "The Atmospheres of the Planets," *Handbuch der Physik*, Vol. LII (1959), p. 404.

6. Sagan, *Organic Matter and the Moon,* p. 23.
7. *Idem.,* "Biological Contamination of the Moon," *Proceedings of the National Academy of Sciences,* 46, 4 (April 1960), p. 398.
8. *Idem., Organic Matter and the Moon,* pp. 13–25.
9. Urey, *op. cit.,* pp. 404–06.
10. Sagan, "The Planet Venus," *Science,* 133 (March 24, 1961), pp. 849-58 and later private communication.
11. Urey, *op. cit.,* p. 386.
12. Sagan, "The Planet Venus," pp. 857–58.
13. Urey, *op. cit.,* pp. 394–95.
14. Hubertus Strughold, "Biological Profile of Mars," AAAS, Dec. 27.
15. *Ibid.*
16. E. J. Hawrylewicz and R. Ehrlich, "Studies With Microorganisms and Plants Under Simulated Martian Environments," AAAS, Dec. 27. Also subsequent discussion.
17. Urey, *op. cit.,* p. 400.
18. Alan E. Nourse, *Nine Planets,* pp. 156–58.
19. Frank B. Salisbury, "Martian Biology," *Science,* 136 (April 6, 1962).
20. Sagan, "On the Origin and Planetary Distribution of Life," *Radiation Research,* 15, 2 (August 1961), pp. 188–89.
21. Isaac Asimov, "By Jove!" *The Magazine of Fantasy and Science Fiction,* 22, 5 (May 1962), p. 64.

Chapter 4

1. Su-Shu Huang, "Life Outside the Solar System," *Scientific American,* 202, 4 (April 1960). See also the same author's "Occurrence of Life in the Universe," *American Scientist,* 47, 3 (Autumn 1959).

Chapter 5

1. Isaac Asimov, "Not As We Know It," *The Magazine of Fantasy and Science Fiction,* 21, 3 (Sept. 1961).
2. *Idem.,* "Planets Have an Air About Them." *Astounding Science Fiction,* 59, 1 (March 1957), p. 104.
3. Hal Clement, *Mission of Gravity,* New York, Doubleday, 1954. See also the same author's article "Whirligig World," *Astounding Science Fiction,* 51, 4 (June 1953).
4. Fred Hoyle, *The Black Cloud,* New York, Harper, 1957.

Chapter 6

1. Leslie Charteris, *The Saint Intervenes*, New York, Triangle Books, 1940, p. 111. By permission of Doubleday & Company, Inc.
2. Weston La Barre, *The Human Animal.*
3. Robert Ardrey, *African Genesis.*
4. Susanne Langer, *Philosophy in a New Key.*
5. L. Sprague de Camp, "Design for Life," *Astounding Science Fiction*, 23, 3–4 (May–June 1939).
6. V. A. Eulach, "Those Impossible Autotrophic Men," *Astounding Science Fiction*, 53, 2 (Oct. 1956).
7. Harry C. Stubbs, "Life Spectra," AAAS, Dec. 27. Published in *Vorpal Glass*, 1, 4 (March 1962).
8. Paul Ash, "Big Sword," *Astounding Science Fiction*, 62, 2 (Oct. 1958).
9. Hal Clement, *Needle*, New York, Doubleday, 1950.
10. Poul Anderson, "Hiding Place," *Analog*, 67, 1 (March 1961).

Chapter 7

1. Clarence Day, *This Simian World.*
2. Charles Galton Darwin, *The Next Million Years.*
3. P. B. Medawar, *The Future of Man.*
4. Much of what follows in this chapter appeared, in a somewhat different form, as part of an article by the present author entitled "Science and Superman: An Inquiry," *Amazing Science Fiction Stories*, 33, 11 (Nov. 1959). Copyright 1959 by Ziff-Davis Publishing Company and used by permission.
5. Roderick Seidenberg, *Prehistoric Man.*
6. Medawar, *op. cit.*, pp. 70–83.

Chapter 8

1. Private communication. But see V. Gordon Childe, *The Dawn of European Civilization*, especially Chapters I and II.
2. Much of what follows in this chapter appeared, in a somewhat different form, as part of an article by the present author entitled "How Social Is Science?" *Saturday Review*, 50, 7 (April 27, 1957). Copyright 1957 by Saturday Review, Inc., and used by permission.
3. John W. Campbell, "Muffed Chances," *Astounding Science Fiction*, 39, 4 (June 1947).
4. See, for example, the chronicle of Anna Comnena.

Chapter 9

1. Giuseppe Cocconi and Philip Morrison, "Searching for Interstellar Communications," *Nature*, 184, 2 (Sept. 19, 1959), pp. 844–46.
2. Sebastian von Hoerner, "The Search for Signals From Other Civilizations," *Science*, 134 (Dec. 8, 1961), p. 1842.
3. *Ibid.*
4. Su-Shu Huang, "Occurrence of Life in the Universe," *American Scientist*, 47, 3 (Autumn 1959).
5. Von Hoerner, *op. cit.*, 1839–43.

Appendix

1. See especially J. R. Pierce in *Proceedings of the Institute of Radio Engineers*, 47, 1053 (1959) and Sebastian von Hoerner in *Science*, 137 (July 6, 1962). Neither of these articles had come to my attention when this appendix was being written.
2. See communication by R. W. Bussard in *Astronautica Acta*, 6, 179 (1960).

Bibliography

THIS LIST is intended to be representative rather than exhaustive. It includes all nonfiction books cited in the text, plus a number of others that I can recommend to anyone interested in these matters. But of course space limitations—and ignorance—have forced me to omit many works that are just as good.

Titles marked (*) are perhaps too technical for the reader without scientific training.

Ardrey, Robert, *African Genesis*, New York, Atheneum, 1961.

Asimov, Isaac, *The Intelligent Man's Guide to Science* (2 vols.), New York, Basic Books, 1960.

———, *The Wellsprings of Life*, New York, Abelard-Schuman, 1960.

Bernal, J. D., *The Physical Basis of Life* (*), London, Routledge, 1951.

Bova, Ben, *The Milky Way Galaxy*, New York, Holt, 1961.

Cameron, Alastair, *Stellar Evolution, Nuclear Astrophysics and Nucleogenesis* (*), Chalk River, Ont., Atomic Energy of Canada, Ltd., Chalk River Project, Research and Development, 1957.

Childe, V. Gordon, *The Dawn of European Civilization* (sixth ed.), New York, Knopf, 1958.

Clarke, Arthur C., *The Challenge of the Spaceship*, New York, Harper, 1959.

———, *The Exploration of Space*, New York, Harper, 1952.

Darwin, Sir Charles Galton, *The Next Million Years*, New York, Doubleday, 1953.

Day, Clarence, *This Simian World*, New York, Knopf, 1920.

Fallone, E. M. (ed.), *Proceedings of Lunar and Planetary Exploration Colloquium* (*), Downey, Calif., North American Aviation, Inc., 1961.

Hoyle, Fred, *Frontiers of Astronomy*, New York, Harper, 1955.

La Barre, Weston, *The Human Animal*, Chicago, University of Chicago, 1954.

Langer, Susanne, *Philosophy in a New Key*, Cambridge, Harvard University, 1957.

Ley, Willy and Bonestell, Chesley, *The Conquest of Space*, New York, Viking, 1949.

Lyttleton, Raymond A., *The Modern Universe*, New York, Harper, 1956.

Medawar, P. B., *The Future of Man*, New York, Basic Books, 1959; New American Library, 1961.

Moore, Patrick, *A Guide to the Moon*, New York, Norton, 1953.

———, *A Guide to the Planets*, New York, Norton, 1954.

Nourse, Alan E., *Nine Planets*, New York, Harper, 1960.

Oparin, A. I., *The Origin of Life on the Earth* (*), 3rd ed., translated by Ann Synge, New York, Academic, 1957.

———, Pasynskii, A. G., Braunshtein, A. E., and Pavlovskaya, T. E. (eds.), *Proceedings of the First International Symposium on the Origin of Life on the Earth* (*). English-French-German ed., New York, Pergamon, 1959.

Ovenden, Michael, *Life in the Universe*, New York, Doubleday, 1962.

Payne-Gaposchkin, Cecilia, *Stars in the Making*, Cambridge, Harvard University, 1952.

Pfeiffer, John, *The Changing Universe*, New York, Random House, 1956.

———, *From Galaxies to Man*, New York, Random House, 1959.

Richardson, R. S., *Exploring Mars*, New York, McGraw, 1954.

Rudaux, Lucien, and de Vaucouleurs, G. (eds.), *Larousse Encyclopedia of Astronomy*, translated by Michael Guest and John B. Sidgwick, revised by Z. Kopal, New York, Prometheus, 1959.

Sagan, Carl, *Organic Matter and the Moon* (*), Washington, National Academy of Sciences—National Research Council (Publication 757), 1961.

Scientific American (eds.), *The Planet Earth*, New York, Simon & Schuster, 1957.

———, *The Universe*, New York, Simon & Schuster, 1957.
Seidenberg, Roderick, *Posthistoric Man*, Chapel Hill, University of North Carolina, 1950.
Shapley, Harlow, *Of Stars and Men*, Boston, Beacon, 1958.
Struve, Otto, *Stellar Evolution* (*), Princeton, Princeton University, 1950.

Urey, Harold C., *The Planets: Their Origin and Development* (*), New Haven, Yale University, 1952.

Whipple, Fred, *Earth, Moon, and Planets*, New York, Grosset, 1958.

Shortly before this revised edition was prepared—too late for me to insert it in its proper place in my bibliography—there appeared a book which I recommend most heartily to everyone interested in the subject:

Shklovskii, I. S., and Sagan, Carl, *Intelligent Life in the Universe*, San Francisco, Holden-Day, 1966.

Glossary

A NOTE ON USAGE: To avoid the irritating effect of repeating the same words in close sequence, I have provided myself with synonyms for some of the commonest by assigning rather special definitions. In one case this leads to a technical inaccuracy—the use of "weight" as equivalent to "mass," and "heavy" as equivalent to "massive"—but I hope the reader will join me in sanctioning these metaphors. The true meaning should always be clear from context. As for the other words, when capitalized, "Sun" (adjective "Solar") refers to Sol, our own sun; in lower case, "sun" (adjective "solar") means any star. Likewise, capitalized "Moon" refers to Luna, the satellite of Earth, whereas "moon" in lower case means any satellite of a planet. A "world" is any solid heavenly body, be it planet or satellite, of reasonable size. It is "inhabited" if it has life upon it, intelligent or not.

The following glossary is not intended for the trained scientist, and I ask him to forgive certain oversimplifications that seemed necessary.

Absolute zero: The lowest possible temperature that matter can reach, when all heat energy has been removed. It is equal to −459.7° F. *Absolute temperature* is reckoned from this point.

Actinic light or *radiation:* Electromagnetic radiation (q.v.) capable of producing chemical changes in matter; usually of fairly short wave length. Cf. *Quantum*.

Allotrope: A particular form, with a distinct molecular organization, in which an element can occur. Thus, diamond, graphite, and lampblack are three different allotropes of carbon.

Anaerobic: Of organisms, active in the absence of free oxygen.

Angular momentum: The quantity of rotation possessed by a body. It is proportional to the mass and the speed of rotatory motion, though the exact shape of the body must also be taken into account.

ATP: Adenosine triphosphate, an organic compound essential to energy transfer within living cells.

Binary star: A double star, i.e., two stars revolving around their common center of gravity.

Carbohydrates: An important class of organic compounds, made up of carbon (C), hydrogen (H), and oxygen (O). It includes the starches and sugars. A typical carbohydrate is the sugar glucose, one form of which has the following molecular structure:

```
           H         H     H
           |         |     |
     O     O    H    O     O    H
     ||    |    |    |     |    |
H ── C ─── C ── C ── C ─── C ── C ── O ── H
           |    |    |     |    |
           H    O    H     H    H
                |
                H
```

Each line in this formula stands for a chemical bond. Note the double bond at the left. The "extra" bond could attach to something else; hence the molecule is unsaturated. (See *Unsaturation.*)

Carbonates: Salts of carbonic acid, H_2CO_3. A typical one is calcium carbonate, $CaCO_3$.

Catalyst: A substance that influences the rate of a chemical reaction without undergoing any net change itself. Some catalysts operate by providing a finely divided surface on which reacting molecules can cluster thickly; some enter into intermediate reactions, being reproduced in their original form by the terminal processes, etc. Without catalysts, many reactions could not take place to any noticeable extent.

Cells: The small, usually microscopic units out of which living organisms are built.

Chromosomes: The threadlike bodies within cells that carry the coded information of heredity.

DNA: Deoxyribonucleic acid, the nucleic acid out of whose various forms the chromosomes are apparently built.

Eccentricity: A geometrical ratio that gives a measure of how far from the circular form (eccentricity zero) an ellipse such as a planetary orbit is.

Ecology: The mutually important relationships between organisms, their environment, and each other; also, any system that exhibits such relationships; also, the study of such relationships.

Electromagnetic radiation: The class of wavelike radiant energy to which light belongs. In free space it travels at the speed of light, with wave length and frequency inversely proportional to each other. The longest wave lengths and lowest frequencies in common use belong to radio waves. Beyond them, in order of decreasing wave length, come infrared radiation, visible light, ultraviolet light, X rays, and gamma rays. Cf. *Quantum.*

Enzyme: Any of a large class of organic catalysts that regulate and make possible the chemical processes within living organisms. Apparently enzyme production is controlled by the genes (q.v.).

Escape velocity: The velocity needed to recede from some point relative to a body (e.g., from the surface of a planet) to an indefinitely great distance. The escape velocity for Earth is seven miles per second. A shell fired from the surface at this speed—neglecting air resistance—would not fall back but would continue outward with steadily diminishing velocity. Of course, an object that can accelerate continuously, such as a rocket, need not start out so fast.

Gene: A unit, apparently a locus on the chromosome (q.v.), that controls some one aspect of the total heredity, evidently by causing the production or nonproduction of a particular enzyme (q.v.).

Heat of evaporation: The amount of heat, in calories, needed to change one gram of a substance at its boiling point from the liquid to the gaseous state.

Heat of fusion: The amount of heat, in calories, needed to change one gram of a substance at its melting point from the solid to the liquid state.

Hydrated: Of compounds, containing water in a loose combination with the rest of the molecule.

Hydrocarbons: Compounds of carbon and hydrogen only. The simplest is methane, CH_4. Cf. *Carbohydrates.*

Hydrosphere: The watery envelope of a planet: oceans, lakes, ground water, water in soil capillaries, etc.

Interferometry: Precision measurement using, as indicators, the bright and dark bands produced when light waves interfere with each other.

Ion: An atom, molecule, or radical (q.v.) that carries a net electrical charge, either positive or negative.

Lipids: A class of organic compounds including fats, oils, and other esters that possess analogous properties.

Magnitude: A measure of the apparent brightness of a star or other celestial object. The *apparent magnitude* is that which we observe from Earth. A star of the first magnitude is about two and one-half times as bright as one of the second magnitude, which in turn is two and one-half times as bright as one of the third magnitude, etc. The Sun is of magnitude −26.7, the faintest naked-eye stars about +6. The *absolute magnitude* is that which a star would have if brought to a standard distance of ten parsecs (32.6 light-years). For the Sun it is 4.85.

Mass: The quantity of matter in a body.

Mutation: A change in the heredity, which is itself inherited: apparently due to the chemical alteration of a gene (q.v.).

Nebula: A great cloud of dust and gas in space, considerably denser than the interstellar medium, though still very tenuous by Earthly standards.

Nucleic acids: A class of organic acids. Cf. *DNA*.

Nucleus: Of an atom, the positively charged central part, which contains nearly all the mass and around which the negative electrons are grouped. Of a cell, the dark central portion in which much of the structure is found. Of a spiral galaxy, the star-crowded central portion from which the arms branch out (see Figs. 1 and 2, Chapter 1).

Organic compounds: Compounds of carbon.

Orogeny: The process of elevating land and forming mountains.

Oxidation: Loosely, any process that increases the proportion of oxygen in a compound. More precisely, that part of a chemical reaction which moves electrons from an atom or molecule, making it more positive electrically. Oxygen oxidizes many substances, but is not the only element that can do so. Cf. *Reduction*.

Parameter: A variable on whose value depends some characteristic of a system.

Photomultiplier: Any device that amplifies the light falling upon it to produce a brighter image.

Polarimeter: A device for measuring the polarization of light.

Polarized light: Light whose properties vary with the direction, at right angles to the line of propagation, in which its waves travel. *Plane polarized* light vibrates in a single plane perpendicular to the direction in which a given ray moves. This plane is rotated when the light passes through a substance whose molecules are asymmetric, e.g., a solution of a single isomer.

Proper motion: A star's apparent angular rate of motion on the celestial sphere, produced by its actual motion with respect to the Sun.

Proteins: A class of complex, nitrogenous organic compounds, a major part of all living cells.

Purines: A class of organic compounds including a pyrimidine (q.v.) and an imidazole ring.

Pyrimidines: A class of organic compounds based on a ring-shaped molecule that includes two nitrogen atoms. They are constituents of certain amino acids.

Pyrroles: A class of organic compounds somewhat similar to the pyrimidines. The pyrrole ring is part of the chlorophyll and hemoglobin molecules.

Quantum: One of the small units or packets of energy in which electromagnetic radiation (q.v.) is given off or absorbed. The higher the frequency of the radiation, i.e., the shorter the wave length, the more energy each of its quanta possesses. Therefore actinic light (q.v.) is of relatively short wave length.

Radical: An incomplete part of a molecule, electrically charged and chemically active. For example, the radicals of the calcium carbonate molecule (see *Carbonates*) are the calcium ion, with two positive charges, and the doubly negative carbonate (CO_3) ion.

Reduction: Loosely, any process that increases the proportion of hydrogen in a compound. More precisely, that part of a chemical reaction which moves electrons to an atom or molecule, making it less positive electrically. Hydrogen reduces many substances but is not the only element which can do so. Cf. *Oxidation.*

Saprophyte: An organism, especially a small one, that lives off dead organisms.

Saturation: In chemistry, the process or state of having atoms (or radicals) attached by all bonds available to the atoms in a molecule. A saturated compound is therefore one that has no way of uniting with anything else except by displacing something to which it is already united. Cf. *Unsaturation.*

Specific heat: A quantity equal to the number of calories required to raise the temperature of one gram of a substance one degree centigrade. The specific heat of water at 15° C. is 1 by definition.

Spectroanalysis: The study of the composition and state of materials by the light coming from them, as separated into its different wave lengths by the spectroscope.

Symbiosis: The close association of two or more different types of organisms to their mutual advantage. Such organisms are called *symbionts.* Man is symbiotic with his intestinal flora—bacteria in the gut—which help him digest his food, and which gain nourishment and shelter as they do.

Telemetry: The use of instruments that send back their readings (usually by radio) to persons or recorders at a distance.

Thermocouple: A device that, converting heat radiation into electricity, can measure the temperature of a distant object.

Thermodynamics: The study of heat and its relationships to matter and to other forms of energy.

Thermonuclear reactions: Reactions that occur between atomic nuclei moving at such high speeds that they fuse or shatter when they collide, thereby producing different nuclei and often releasing energy.

Unsaturation: In chemistry, the process or state of having atoms (or radicals) attached by fewer bonds than are available to the atoms in a molecule. An unsaturated compound can therefore unite with other materials without displacing anything already present. Cf. *Carbohydrates* and *Saturation.*

Index

www.ingramcontent.com/pod-product-compliance
Lightning Source LLC
Chambersburg PA
CBHW061730270326
41928CB00011B/2182
9781955087155